Echoes

from the Valley

– ¦ –

By Billy Powell

Indigo Custom Publishing, LLC

Publisher	Henry S. Beers
Associate Publisher	Richard J. Hutto
Executive Vice President	Robert G. Aldrich
Operations Manager	Gary G. Pulliam
Editor-in-Chief	Joni Woolf
Art Director/Designer	Julianne Gleaton
Designer	Daniel Emerson
Director of Marketing and Public Relations	Mary D. Robinson

Printed in U.S.A.

Library of Congress Control Nmber: 2006931163

ISBN: (10 Digit) 1-934144-00-2   ISBN: (13 Digit) 978-1-934144-00-8

Indigo Custom Publishing, LLC books are available at quantity discounts with bulk purchase for educational, business, or sales promotional use.

For information, please write to:
Indigo Custom Publishing, LLC • SunTrust Bank Building • 435 Second St. • Suite 320 • Macon, GA 31201, or call toll free 866-311-9578.

Cover image courtesy of: **Historic Pineola Farms** - Peach County, Ga. Paul & Delise Knight www.pineola.com

Dedication

First and foremost, I dedicate this book to the glory of God. Without His guiding hand and timely intervention at critical stages, this book would not have been possible.

Secondly, this book is dedicated to my wife, Beverly Davis Powell, who painstakingly proofread and edited my drafts page-by-page and provided invaluable insight and counsel toward making this book the best product it could possibly be.

Thirdly, *Echoes from the Valley* is dedicated to my two sons and daughters-in-law, Bill and Cindy Powell, and Tim and Judy Powell, who have provided encouragement and inspiration at every step along the way.

And finally, it is dedicated to my grandchildren who have enthusiastically supported their granddaddy in this endeavor:

Ashtyn Powell

Alyssa Powell

Jacob Powell

Eli Powell

Jordan Powell

Acknowledgments

I am deeply indebted to seven individuals who have shared extensively with me their remembrances of bygone days in the Valley. These individuals, considered the top local historians, grew up in the Valley, have lived here all their lives, and possess an encyclopedic recall of our storied past: its people, its places, and its events. Among this "magnificent seven" resides the collective knowledge of life in the Valley during the twentieth century. This book would not have been possible without their input.

Fred Shepard

Wallis Hardeman

Judge George B. Culpepper III

Marcus Hickson Jr.

Buddy Luce

Billy Marshall

Calvin Mason

Others who have provided immeasurable assistance:

Marilyn Windham: history and photos of the 1922-1926 Peach festivals.
Henry Outler: assistance in identifying Peach County veterans of World Wars I and II.
Dr. Donnie Bellamy: history and photos of Fort Valley State University.
Evelyn McCray: history of Henry A. Hunt High School.
Vickie Davis: *"Leader Tribune"* archives and Peach County newspaper history.
Gilda Stanberry-Cotney: Peach County library history.
Dorothy Hudson: historical information from archives of Fort Valley Historical Society.
Joyce Mason: historical research and documentation on a wide range of topics.
Naomi Simmons: yearbooks of Fort Valley High School and Peach County High School.
Jana Jones: information on theater and freight depot restorations and various photos.
Sarah Anne Maffett: Macon County history.
Virginia Clark Howard and **Tom Turner:** Magazine articles on the Possum Trot murder.
Fort Valley Police Chief John Anderson and **Assistant District Attorney Wayne "Biff" Tillis:** their cooperation in making available the case files on the Denise Allison murder.

Indigo Custom Publishing LLC: My appreciation to Indigo Custom Publishing Company, a class act with a highly professional and skilled staff: Henry Beers, Gary Pulliam, Joni Woolf, Mary Robinson, Rick Hutto, Daniel Emerson, Julianne Gleaton, and Nick Malloy.

Table of Contents

Foreword

A few weeks ago, my five-year-old daughter asked me if we could go to the "graveyard." Curious about what she was interested in, I took her out to Oaklawn Cemetery and we looked around a while. After visiting the family graves and answering her questions as best I could about the Culpeppers, Shepards, and Vances, we rode around a while and looked at the different types of headstones and the names of the folks buried there.

Among the thousands laid to rest at Oaklawn are peach farmers, soldiers, business owners, preachers, lawyers, sheriffs, Blue Bird people, Woolfolk people, railroad men, and even a few politicians. Some were prominent persons and have fine memorials. Others, long forgotten, have only a crumbling slab with no inscription and no name.

There are the small stone lambs marking the graves of so many babies and children who died with illnesses that medical science has long since cured. Next to them were later buried their mothers and fathers.

All of them had stories to tell. There were stories of successes, stories of failures, and stories of fortunes made and fortunes lost. Their words spoke of the early times, the beginnings, and the building of our town. There were stories of faith and stories of compassion. There were stories that made us proud and heart-rending stories that touched our hearts.

And now, like the story tellers, so many of the recollections are gone. Their stories were buried with them. Fortunately, Billy Powell has saved for us a precious few.

We are privileged that Billy Powell has spent so many hours in research and study to produce this volume of work. He has extensively read, and listened and written. We are the beneficiaries of this effort.

In this book Billy paints a picture, "warts and all," of our community. In his writings he conveys a deep sense of appreciation for our history and a reverence for those who once lived where we live.

Over the years Billy Powell has come to love Fort Valley. That's no small accomplishment for a man from Perry.

This work will enlighten us, inform us, and inspire our children. Hopefully, it will encourage us to not let those who follow us wonder who we were.

Bryant Culpepper
Superior Court Judge: 1983 to present
Georgia House of Representatives: 1975-1982

Chapter 1

FOUNDING OF FORT VALLEY, BYRON, POWERSVILLE, AND THE CREATION OF PEACH COUNTY

Creek Indian Territory: Prior to 1821

The Creek Indians, who fought against the United States in the Creek War of 1813-1814, roamed the land that is now Fort Valley. This area had been a vast hunting ground for the Indians. The entire region, which became Houston County, extended from the Flint River (west) to the Ocmulgee River (east) and from Fort Hawkins-Macon (north) to Old Hartford-Hawkinsville (south). Following the treaty with the Creek Indians in 1821, the Creeks migrated westward, eventually to Oklahoma.

Everett's Trading Post: 1820s

James Abington Everett (1788-1848) moved here from North Carolina early in his life. During the 1820s, he established a trading post at the intersection of two major Indian trails: (1) extending from Fort Hawkins in Macon to Barnard's Crossing near Montezuma, and (2) from the Creek Indian Agency north of Reynolds to Old Hartford near Hawkinsville.

Painting of James Abington Everett.

Fort Valley Moved From Crawford County

The first Fort Valley post office was established inside Crawford County—on the Atlanta Highway on December 7, 1825, with James A. Everett as the first postmaster. The first settlers other than Everett were Mathew Dorsey (co-donor of Everett Square), Peter Greene (Everett's father-in-law), William Wiggins and son Allen Wiggins (Billy Marshall's great-great-grandfather). In a letter to Thelma Wilson (beloved local teacher), W. H. Harris wrote: "The post office of Fort Valley was originally in Crawford County. The county lines didn't move... but Fort Valley moved. It was originally about two miles out on the Atlanta Highway." In 1834, Everett transferred the post office from his house in Crawford County to his downtown store in Fort Valley.

Also, in 1834, Everett built a house (oldest in Peach County) less than a mile east of the original Crawford County post office, just across the line into Houston County. There he lived until his death. Later it became Jeane's Antique Shop. Judge Bryant Culpepper purchased the house in 1982, moved it to 300 Northwoods Drive, and restored it.

James A. Everett's house circa 1960. Photo courtesy Jann Culpepper.

"Fox" or "Fort" Valley

There was never a fort or a valley in this area. Being 525 feet above sea level, Fort Valley sits on an elevated ridge extending from Augusta to Cuthbert. W. H. Harris facetiously wrote in the *Leader Tribune* in 1924: "We have here a valley set upon a hill, where a fort ought to be."

Fort Valley was located on a strip of cleared land about one mile wide and twelve miles long, representing the appearance of a valley where red fox were hunted. Hunters dubbed the settlement "Fox Valley."

In 1825 when application was made for a post office, the Post Office Department in Washington--due to poor handwriting--misread the intended name "Fox" Valley as "Fort" Valley. This misinterpretation possibly was attributed to flourishes in marking the "X".

Others contend that Everett named the town after his friend, Arthur Fort, a Revolutionary War hero and Milledgeville legislator. The town should have been named Everettville.

Fort Valley Chartered: 1856

Fort Valley was chartered by the state legislature on March 3, 1856. Dr. William Asbury Mathews, Houston County representative, introduced the bill. The corporate limits were set one mile from the railroad depot. Appointed as commissioners and empowered to make laws were: C. D. Anderson, William H. Hollinshead, William I. Greene, A. D. Kendrick, and D. N. Austin. These five served until their successors were named. The names of the first elected officials are not known.

Prior to 1953, when the present City Hall was completed, city government was administered from the Water and Light Plant, south of the Harris House (later named Winona Hotel) located on South Main Street next to railroad.

Contributions of James A. Everett

James A. Everett first married Cussena Barnard, daughter of Timpoochie Barnard, a Creek Indian leader and signer of the 1825 treaty of Indian Springs (remainder of Indian land not obtained by U.S. in 1821 treaty) This ensured Everett's welcome among the Indians and granted him ownership of a large reserve at the signing of the treaty. His second wife was Mary Beaufort Greene, daughter of Peter Beaufort and Sarah (Ingram) Greene. At his death in 1848, Everett owned 12,144.5 acres of land, 242 slaves, and an estate valued at half-a-million dollars (in 1848 dollars). In 1850, Everett's widow, Mary, married Dr. William Asbury Mathews, who introduced the legislation to charter Fort Valley in 1856.

In 1836, Everett and Mathew Dorsey deeded six acres of land for school and church purposes. Built on Everett Square were: Fort Valley Academy-1836, Wesley Manual Labor School for boys-1837, Fort Valley Methodist Church-1848, Fort Valley Consolidated School-1912, and Fort Valley Primary School-1952. Everett's signal contribution was purchasing fifty thousand dollars in railroad stock and luring the Georgia Southwestern Railroad to come through Fort Valley. The railroad was completed in 1851, three years after his death. The railroad opened up the opportunity for Fort Valley to transport its peaches to northern markets on refrigerated cars, thus Fort Valley became the "Peach Capital of the World" and during 1922-1926 organized the matchless Peach Festivals that annually drew forty to fifty thousand visitors to the community.

Everett was buried three times: first buried near the old freight depot, later moved to an area overlooking Everett Square, and finally interred in Oaklawn Cemetery, which he had given to the city.

Gravesite of James A. Everett, 1788-1848, (left) and wife, Mary, 1824-1852, (right) in Fort Valley's Oaklawn Cemetery. Not pictured, but to right of Mary's grave is marker of Henry P. Everett, son of James A. Everett, who fought in Civil War as member of the 57th Georgia Infantry.

Fort Valley Mayors: 1888-Present

A. C. Riley: 1888-90, J. L. Fincher: Jan-Apr 1890 (unexpired term of Riley who resigned), J. M. Houser:1890-92, O. M. Houser:1892-94, A D. Skellie: 1894-1904, J. L. Fincher: 1904-10, J. W. Rundell:1910-12, O. M. Houser:1912-14, J. R. Kinney:1914-16, A. B. Greene:1916-18, H. C. Neil:1918-22, A. C. Riley Jr.: 1922-24, R. D. Hale:1924-26 (unexpired second term of Riley, who resigned), H. M. Copeland:1926-28, Dr. W. S. White: 1928-32, Glenmore Green:1932-42, A. C. Riley Jr.: 1942-48, T. A. McCord: 1948-54, D. N. Wells: Apr-Dec 1954 (interim term until Marion Allen reached twenty-fifth birthday), Marion Allen: 1954-58, Irving Rigdon:1958-62, Ann Frances Vinson:1962-64 (first female mayor), David I. Sammons: 1964-70, Paul Rheeling:1970-80, Rudolph Carson:1980-82, C. W. Peterson:1982-94, Dr. Jimmy L. Williams:1994-96, John W. Ezell Jr.:1996-98, and John E. Stumbo:1998 to present.

Mayor J. L. Fincher brought electricity and water to Fort Valley homes.

Millard Moseley, first ordinary and county manager of Peach County; from Byron, Georgia.

Mayor John Stumbo brought unity and community spirit to Fort Valley, Georgia.

Incorporation of Byron: 1874

A settlement existed in Byron as early as 1820. The Byron area was identified as "Bateman" on maps until 1874. During the early 1850s, Byron became a flag stop on the Southwestern Railroad. The railroad named it Station Number One and One-Half. It maintained a wood rack for wood-burning engines with no provision for supplying water to the trains (the trains stopped at Powersville, six miles down the track, for water). Since Nimrod Jackson operated the station, the railroad flag stop was named after him and became known as Jackson Station. Thus, the community that would become Byron was referred to as Jackson Station from around 1850 until 1874.

4

Dr. C. H. Richardson, a South Carolinian, settled there after the Civil War. Through his efforts, the area called Jackson Station (identified on maps as Bateman) was incorporated as Byron on March 3, 1874. The townspeople wanted to name the town "Richardsonville" after the beloved Dr. Richardson, but Richardson opted to name the town Byron in honor of Lord Byron, the colorful English poet (1788-1824). Dr. Richardson became Byron's first Mayor in 1874.

Byron's Founder:
Dr. C. H. Richardson.

Byron Mayors: 1908-Present

C.C. Richardson: 1908-09, Columbus M. Dupree: 1910-11, W. G. Southall: 1912-13, Charles L. Bateman: 1914-16, Charles H. Jackson: 1916-20, Millard C. Moseley: 1921 (interim term), George P. Cline: 1922-27, W. Durwood Aultman: 1927-40, Robert L. Murdock: 1940-53, Henry J. Williams: 1953-61, W. Edwin Green Jr.: 1961-75, Lawrence C. Collins: 1976-83, James E. Williams: 1984-99, Robert D. Wright: 2000-03, Lawrence C. Collins: 2004 – Present.

The Flag Stop South of Byron: Powersville

On the 1874 map, the Powersville and Byron areas were identified only as "Bateman." These two communities sprang up along the railroad and became flag stops between Macon and Fort Valley.

During the late 1840s, the Southwestern Railroad established a wood and water station six miles down the track from Jackson Station called Station Number Two. Echeeconee was station #1, Jackson Station (later to become Byron) was station #1 and one half, and what would become Powersville was station #2. The water came from Mule Creek and the wood was cut and sold to the railroad by Mr. Buck Warren. Mr. Alfred W. Cliett suggested the community be named Powersville in honor of Colonel Virgil Powers, superintendent of the Southwestern Railroad Company. Richard Cuyler was railroad president. Subsequently, the post office at Bateman's store was moved to the railroad stop at Powersville where William E. Warren acted as both postmaster and railway agent.

Later when the railroad became the Central of Georgia, the Central provided a steam pump and two huge water towers—a more convenient way to provide water than the "bucket brigade" from Mule Creek. Mr. Tom Cliett was pumper for the Central for years. In 1881, Powersville had two stores and five white residences. Later came a grist mill, a cotton gin, and several saw mills. At one point in its early history, Powersville boasted of being the Watermelon Center of the world.

Creation of Peach County: 1924

The struggle to create Peach County began in the Georgia General Assembly in 1916. Legislation passed the Senate but not the House. In 1922, Senator Joseph E. Davidson of Fort Valley and state representatives C. H. Jackson of Byron and Emmett Houser of Perry succeeded in having both houses pass the legislation, but it failed at ratification in the general referendum. In 1924, all sides got together again and drew the proposed county lines (151 square miles of land were taken from Houston and Macon Counties). Senator G. E. Smith of the 23rd District introduced the measure. In the Referendum of November 7, 1924, it was ratified by a vote of three to one.

Governor Thomas W. Hardwick signs bill creating Peach County. Looking on L-R: Emmett Houser, legislator who wrote the bill; Charles H. Jackson, legislator of Byron; H. C. Neil, Fort Valley mayor; and Joe E. Davidson, legislator who presented bill.

Peach County (named after its peaches) officially began on January 1, 1925. The first county officers were: Joseph E. Davidson, representative in the General Assembly; Millard C. Mosely, Byron, ordinary; Emmett Houser, Clerk of Superior Court; George D. Anderson, sheriff; Dr. W. Haslam Hafer, coroner; T. E. Tharpe, Byron, tax collector; C. N. Roundtree, tax receiver; C. E. Martin, treasurer; and Thomas F. Flournoy, surveyor.

The ordinary served as county manager. The first ordinary was Millard C. Mosely of Byron. He was followed by Bernard A. Young and Julian F. Jones. During Jones's tenure, a legislative act dated March 10, 1964, created an elective board of three commissioners to manage the county. Forty years later, Peach County now has five county commissioners with James Khoury as chairman. Another early change was the merger of tax collector and tax receiver under the office of tax commissioner.

Sources: *History of Peach County Georgia*
The Leader Tribune
Fort Valley and Byron City governments
Internet articles

Chapter 2
Peach Capital of the World

Origin of Peaches

"Prunus persica," the scientific name of the peach, suggests that peaches came from Persia, but China is widely held to be the native home of peaches with archaeological evidence dating back to 4000 B.C. The peach was brought to Europe from Iran and Japan. By 300 B.C., the peach was known in Greece. Shortly after 100 A.D., the peach was introduced to the Romans. The Spanish brought peaches to America. Today, the peach is grown in over sixty countries worldwide. The U.S. produces about 20 percent of the world's peaches.

Peaches Grown in Georgia

Peaches were first grown in Georgia during the colonial period of the 1700s. After the Civil War, Georgia growers developed several hardy varieties that boosted the commercial peach industry and made Georgia the "Peach State." During 1870-75, Samuel Henry Rumph, at his Willow Lake Plantation three miles east of Marshallville, developed the most popular peach, the Elberta, named after his wife. The Elberta became highly successful on northern markets because of its exceptional color, size, overall quality, and the ability to withstand rail shipment without significant bruising.

Georgia now produces more than forty varieties of peaches, which are divided into two categories: freestone and clingstone. The fruit of the freestone readily breaks away from the pit, while the clingstone adheres to the pit. Fresh Georgia peaches are available sixteen weeks each year, from mid-May to early August. Central Georgia possesses about 70 percent of the peach trees and produces 83 percent of the state's peaches. South Georgia owns about 25 percent of the trees and produces 12 percent of the state's harvest. Although called the Peach State, Georgia actually ranks third in peach production behind California and South Carolina.

Peach County's Early Peach History

Peach County, once known as a "Peach Paradise," was the last county created in Georgia. It split away from Houston and Macon Counties in 1924. As early as 1825, James Abington Everett (1788-1848; a North Carolina native) set up a trading post at the convergence of two Native American trails. He named the settlement Fort Valley. It was incorporated in 1856. Everett contributed greatly to the development of Fort Valley by donating land and money for the building of churches and schools. He also persuaded the Southwestern Railroad Company to run its rails to Fort Valley from Macon. The first train arrived in 1851. Soon, peach trees were being planted. By the early 1920s, one-third of Georgia's peaches were grown in Fort Valley. In fact, Fort Valley was the hub of the peach industry with over sixteen million trees planted within a one hundred mile radius of town.

The advent of refrigerated boxcars gave the peach industry its biggest boost. In 1925, the Atlantic Ice and Coal Company was built beside the railroad tracks in Fort Valley. It produced large blocks of ice that were loaded into insulated cars to keep the peaches fresh during rail shipment. The first year the company sold 50,000 tons of ice to cool 17,200 cars filled with peaches. This innovation opened up northern markets for the local peach growers.

Peach Blossom Festivals

Marilyn Neisler Windham authored an outstanding book entitled: *Peach County: The World's Peach Paradise*. Published in 1997 by Arcadia Publishing, the book would be an invaluable addition to anyone's library. It contains detailed accounts and photos of the individual Peach Blossom Festivals (1922-1926), plus rare scenes of old Fort Valley, its homes, churches, schools, and downtown businesses.

Marilyn Windham displays her book.

There were five peach festivals, 1922 to 1926. The attendance ranged from thirty to fifty thousand people annually, many from distant places. The railroads brought people from Atlanta, Macon, and outlying cities. Also converging on Fort Valley were governors, legislators, military officers, railroad executives, and other leaders. In 1925, Hollywood studios and *National Geographic* magazine sent crews to film and photograph the events. In 1926, Atlanta's WSB radio station broadcast the pageant. Over the five-year span a total of 185,000 people attended.

Everyone came to view the vast sea of peach blossoms throughout the countryside, to eat free barbeque, to hear bands play, to watch aerial stunt planes perform, to witness downtown parades, and to attend the breath-taking pageants. During that era, Albert James Evans (1875-1949), called "The Peach King," was the premier peach grower.

The pageants were presented in the Oakland Heights area of Fort Valley from 1922 through 1924. Forty acres of land were secured in 1925 north of Blue Bird and an amphitheater built to seat fourteen thousand attendees. In 1926, the water tower was removed from Fincher's Park, where the gazebo now stands, to improve the view for the spectacular parade featuring marching bands, floats, and decorated cars.

Leading ladies in 1924 pageant. Among them were Miss Gladys Slappey, Mrs. J.W. Rundell, Miss Ruth Houser, Miss Mary Belle Houser, Miss Wilma Orr, Miss Helen Marshall, Miss Audrey Fagan, Mrs. Robert Marchman, Mrs. John Allen, Miss Thelma Wilson, Miss Elizabeth Everett, and their pages, kneeling, L-R: Mildred Kendrick and Ruth Howard McMillan.

The highlight of the pageant was coronation of a festival king and queen. The king and queen of the 1922 festival was R .S. Braswell (my great uncle) and Thelma Wilson, who became a revered teacher at Fort Valley High School. Braswell became ill and was replaced by Dr. A. J. Titus. The pageant was called

King and Queen of the 1922 Festival: Dr. A. J. Titus and Miss Thelma Wilson.

"The Sun Goddess." The king, queen, and their court paraded through the peach orchard as heralds trumpeted the arrival of royalty. In 1925, the coronation was held underneath the water tank at Fincher's Park. In 1926, the king and queen, John and Arline Allen, rode to the amphitheater in a beautifully decorated float drawn by six horses. Their royal court and entourage wore Louis XV style costumes. Allen farmed 2,500 acres in peaches.

Each year following the coronation, a large cast—that grew from two hundred actors in 1922 to fifteen hundred in 1926—presented a play in an open-air theater. The annual plays presented the story of the peach—whose origin predates the Savior's birth—and its migration from other countries of the world to America. Some actors in the pageant were dressed as gods and goddesses; others wore the attire of people from foreign countries where the peach originated. The costumes were designed by Miss Lucy Finney and handmade by local women. Some were rented from the wardrobes of Hollywood stars. Mrs. Etta Carithers Houston originated the festival concept, Mrs. Mabel Swartz Withoft authored the pageants, and Miss Pauline Eaton Oak directed them.

Preparations for the barbeque began several days before. Hog carcasses were placed over furnace-like pits fueled by hickory wood to give the meat a distinctive flavor. In 1924, six pits, each six hundred feet long, were dug for the cooking of four hundred hogs. For two full days the process continued with the help of six hundred men. Fifty thousand pounds of barbeque were served. To keep the pork

Hog carcasses were cooked in pits six hundred feet long.

fresh before cooking, it was kept iced down in refrigerated boxcars. J. L. Everett (grandson of James Abington Everett, Fort Valley's founder) was in charge of barbeque preparations. Brunswick stew, bread, pickles, and other accessory dishes were served up in abundance.

The 1924 festival manager was Charles Leighton Shepard. Its sponsor was the Kiwanis Club whose president was E.T. Murray. General David Shanks, Fort McPherson, was the main speaker. The *Leader Tribune*, March 20, 1924, printed the schedule of events and a detailed program for the pageant, listing the principal actors in the play. Two weeks later, on April 3, the *Leader Tribune* reported: "A full 50,000 people attended the third annual Peach Blossom Festival."

Over the course of five years, 1922-1926, the festivals proved progressively more costly and labor intensive. Beginning in 1925, to help defray elevating expenses, tickets to the pageant were sold for one dollar and barbeque tickets for fifty cents a plate. However, by 1927 signs of disenchantment were creeping in. Voluntarism among the townspeople was lacking. The annual cost of festival had reached a burdensome fifty thousand dollars. Further damaging was a declining market as more states began growing peaches. Consequently, the inevitable decision was made to discontinue the annual festivals. The parades, the barbeques, and the pageants were gone forever, yet the magic of those five magnificent years lived on. Marilyn Windham, in her book, described it this way: "For five years they had made a small, unknown, rural community 'The World's Peach Paradise.'"

Fort Valleyans Reminisce About 1920s Festivals

Mildred Kendrick Mathews: "I remember the first queen, Thelma Wilson. She was attractive, intelligent, regal, and poised. She became an outstanding local English teacher. In those days a vast sea of pink peach blossoms spanned from Byron to Marshallville."

Marcus Hickson Jr.: "My dad, Dr. Hickson, and mother, Louise Fagan Hickson, took me to the festival when I was six years old. The last pageant was

Mildred Kendrick Mathews was a performer in the 1920s Peach pageants.

held off Highway 49 in the valley just past Blue Bird. Mr. Jack Duke once had a sawmill down in that bottom."

Wallace Hardeman: "My classmate, Tom Flournoy Jr., and I were actors in a pageant. We were pages to Mrs. Noble Bassett, who acted out the role of France. I once saw a film at the Peach Theater on the 1926 peach festival. Fifteen years ago, the film was found stored in a canister. It had to be destroyed, since old films are highly flammable."

Martha Carithers Rhodes (resides in Smyrna): "My sister, Etta Carithers Houston, originated the idea for the festivals. Miss Pauline Oak, the pageant director, stayed in our home. I served in

1922 pageant as a flower girl to the queen. I was six then. They turned out school for us to practice the plays. Some of us acted as rain drops; others were dancers."

Fred Shepard: "I played the role of a Chinaman in one of pageants at the age of six. One year they constructed a huge mountain called Mount Olympus as a backdrop for the pageant. The Central of Georgia railroad started running special passenger trains to bring visitors to the festivals."

Billy Marshall: "My mother (Idel Wooddall), grandmother (Viloula Wooddall), and aunt (Helen Marshall) were active participants in the 1922-26 pageants."

Former Peach Packing Sheds/Businesses and their locations:

During the early years, peach packing sheds proliferated around Fort Valley. Few structures are still standing. My appreciation to Fred Shepard, Bill Pearson, Bob Marchman, and Wallace Hardeman for helping compile this list, which may exclude some outlying sheds. The names of the sheds–at that time–and approximate locations/landmarks are as follows:

- Pearson's (four sheds): (1) Willard &Lawton–Food Max (2) Irvin–North end of Valley View Dr.
  (3) Walter Thomas Pearson (Bill Pearson's grandfather)–Rackley's Pecan Shed off Peggy Drive (4) Lawton–Lee Pope.
- Smisson's: Citizens Bank
- Marchman's: West side of Usher's Temple near railroad tracks
- Wilson's: Between Anderson Avenue & Knoxville St., near railroad tracks
- Evans/Star Packing Company: CVS Pharmacy
- John David Duke's/Lane's: Hilton Smith's Cabinet Shop
- Maxwell Murray & Dave Strother's: Sun Mark Bank
- John and Leman Duke's: Across tracks from Bypass Bridge
- Edgar Duke's: West of Anthoine's Machine Works
- Wright and Solomon: Jolly Nut
- Hale and Baird's: Where Buckeye Rd. dead-ends–on 'north side' of highway 96 east
- Miami Valley: Highway 96 east, on Bill Davidson's Farm
- Cleveland's: Highway 341 north; behind Grover Cleveland's house
- Tribble's: Zenith, Georgia

- Peach Canning Plant: Church's Fried Chicken
- Atlantic Ice & Coal Company: two separate plants: (1) East of Jolly Nut; across railroad tracks was the distribution plant and (2) across tracks from Blue Bird was the plant where the ice was made.

Hale and Baird's Packing House beside railroad in 1925.

Blocks of ice being loaded on refrigerated cars at Atlantic Ice and Coal Company in 1925.

Peach Industry in Peach County today

The principal peach growers in Peach County are Lane Packing Company on Highway 96 east of Fort Valley and the Big 6 Farm on Zenith Road. Others with acreage in Peach County are Taylor Orchards, Dickey Farms, Barbour Farms, Harris Sledge, and William Brown. Frank Funderburk, County Extension Agent, reported that Peach County had 6,003 acres in commercial peaches in 2005 compared to 6,100 in 2003. The peach production for 2005 was fifty million pounds—this is a 22 percent reduction since 2003 with 64.5 million pounds. However, Peach County now has approximately 660 thousand peach trees—fifty thousand more than in 2003, indicating more trees have been planted to bolster future production.

Present Day Georgia Peach Festival

After a sixty-one-year hiatus since 1926, the annual peach festival was re-instituted in 1987, but not of the size and scope of the 1922-26 festivals. The current festival concept was conceived and set into motion by Mike Lovvorn, former editor of the *Leader Tribune*, and Calvin Mason, a local businessman. It is now called the Georgia Peach Festival and is held annually during the second weekend in June. Attendance for the weekend event averages approximately 15,000 visitors. Featured are such attractions as music, dancing, and fireworks in Fort Valley and Byron; a 5-K road race on Saturday morning in Fort Valley, a band in downtown Fort Valley on Saturday night, arts and crafts booths along Church Street in Fort Valley, and the world's largest peach cobbler served up at the Peach County Courthouse. Although present day peach festivals cannot match the magnitude and grandeur of the 1920s festivals, and current peach production falls short of yesteryears, Fort Valley will always be known as the "Peach Capital of the World."

Sources:

Peach County, The World's Peach Paradise by Marilyn Neisler Windham

Interviews with local citizens

Internet articles

Chapter 3
Early Days of the Railroad

Railroad comes to Fort Valley

The railroad was non-existent in Georgia three decades before the Civil War; however, during the 1830s the Georgia Legislature established railroad companies in major cities. In 1833, the Central of Georgia Railroad was chartered to build railroad connections from the port city of Savannah into the interior of the state. By 1844, the Central of Georgia had constructed a rail link between Savannah and Macon. The fare from Macon to Savannah –a twelve-hour trip–was eight dollars for adults and half price for children. In 1845, the Central of Georgia was instrumental in forming the Southwestern Railroad that brought railroads to southwest Georgia. At that time much interest was generated in running the railroad south from Macon. The civil engineer who made the survey considered Perry the preferred route, but Perry citizens didn't want the railroad, so through Fort Valley it came.

Stock certificates were purchased by thirty citizens such as James Abington Everett, George H. Slappey, Conrad Murph, Mathew Dorsey, William Anderson, and Williamson Mims (writer's great-great-great-grandfather). James Everett (1788-1848) purchased fifty thousand dollars worth of stock, by far the most of any subscriber. He also donated to the new railroad company the land for the depot and the right of way though Fort Valley.

Although Everett was credited with securing the rail system for Fort Valley, he did not live to see its arrival. He died in 1848, before the tracks of the Southwestern reached Fort Valley. At his request, Everett was buried on the railroad right of way near the future site of the freight depot that was built in 1868. Everett was later re-interred near Everett Square and finally placed in Oaklawn Cemetery.

In 1851, three years after Everett's death, the first train came to Fort Valley from Macon. Byron and Powersville became flag-stops for the Southwestern Railroad. Mrs. J. A. Flournoy Jr. of Fort Valley rode on that first train.

In later years, she spoke of riding in an open flat car and of a lavish barbeque dinner served to the crowd, who had assembled to celebrate the railroad's arrival and to witness the spectacle of the first train coming to the Valley.

Railroad spur built to Perry

According to Judge George Culpepper, a spur, 13.5 miles long, from Fort Valley to Perry, was completed in 1873. This line accommodated not only lawyers and others engaged in business of the courts—Fort Valley was part of Houston County then and Perry was the county seat—but also

Judge Culpepper displays famous trains.

transported supplies and farm produce, including peaches and watermelons. Culpepper recalled that the Ice Plant, a half-mile north of downtown Fort Valley and constructed in 1925, provided ice for cooling the boxcars carrying peaches.

The railroad stop between Fort Valley and Perry was Myrtle (near Norwood Springs Road). It featured a general store, post office, and school. Across the tracks from Myrtle was Norwood Springs, with its sulfur spring water. While sitting outside the Myrtle country store in 1925, Fred Shepard witnessed the conductor toss off a rolled-up copy of a newspaper as the train–coming from Perry–rolled slowly by. A railroad engineer once let Shepard drive the train from Myrtle to Fort Valley. Judge Culpepper revealed that the 'passenger line' to Perry was discontinued during the 1930s and that a bus line was established. "The bus parked behind the old Dixie Seafood building on the corner of Miller Street and Marshallville highway…the concrete slabs whereon the bus parked are still there," stated Culpepper.

During the Civil War

During 1861-1865, trains passing through Fort Valley transported soldiers to the front lines and brought back the wounded. Union prisoners passed through Fort Valley enroute to Andersonville. New recruits boarded the train as loved ones waved goodbye and prayed for their safe return. My great-grandfather, Robert Braswell, and his two brothers, Willam and Samuel, were members of the "Everett Guard" that were dispatched from Fort Valley in October 1861 to defend Savannah. Later in 1864, Robert, a member of the 57th Georgia Infantry, was sent by rail from Fort Sumter to the battlefields of Virginia. Passing non-stop through Fort Valley, Robert threw a kiss to the love of his life, Laura Love, who was standing at the Fort Valley station and waving. Later Robert and his brothers fought in the Battle of Atlanta. His two brothers were killed in action, but Robert survived, married Laura Love, and settled in Fort Valley.

After the Civil War

After the Civil War, circa 1886, Fort Valley became the "Southern Terminus" of the Atlanta and Florida Railroad. Railroad traffic rapidly increased over the decades that followed. During the 1930s and 1940s, Judge Culpepper estimated that twenty-two passenger trains came through Fort Valley daily. "There were probably an equal number of freight trains each day," he said. Judge Culpepper related that he had made five transcontinental trips by rail, from one end of the country to the other. He still owns a 1964 Railroad Guide that reflects all rail routes in the United States. For a given train trip, a town-by-town itinerary is shown. Culpepper remembers four fast passenger trains that traveled through Fort Valley during the late 1930s, 1940s, and 1950s: Flamingo, Dixie Flyer, Dixie Limited, and Southland (the fastest). "On a straight stretch these trains would travel seventy-five to eighty miles an hour," he stated. "These passenger locomotives pulled sixteen cars, which included pullmans, observation coaches, a dining car, an express car for parcels, and a mail car with letter drop." During that era, a traveler from Fort Valley could ride the train to Cincinnati, to Chicago, to St. Louis, or to any major city in the United States. According to Culpepper, the 'passenger line' through Fort Valley was discontinued during the late 1960s. Today, there are six to eight freight trains that pass through Fort Valley daily. Rep. Robert Ray was instrumental in construction of the overpass bridge over the railroad to ensure that trains blocking the tracks will not delay ambulances, fire trucks, and emergency vehicles.

Railroad landmarks

Visitors entering Fort Valley from the south immediately realize this town was formerly a railroad community. Near the railroad tracks—at the south end of Main Street—are three old railroad structures that are still standing:

- Freight Depot where rail shipments were unloaded for such former businesses as H.V. Kell Company, Happy Vale Flour Mill, and Woolfork Chemical Plant. The first freight depot was built in 1868; the year after a disastrous fire destroyed

17

the Fort Valley business district. It mysteriously burned to the ground two years later in 1870 and was replaced in 1871, according to Central of Georgia records.

- Passenger Station where passengers purchased tickets and boarded trains-built circa 1907.
- Switching Tower/Telegraph Office-built circa 1907.
- Water Tower & Pumping Station (no longer exist): Judge Culpepper disclosed that near the old Freight Depot were a water tower and pumping station that supplied water to fill trains. One watering station was located at the end of Main Street in front of the old Winona Hotel and the other at the end of East Church Street.

L-R: Railroad freight depot, switching tower/telegraph office, and passenger station.

Hotels

Three former hotels housed railroad travelers: (1) Winona Hotel (on Main Street, next to tracks), (2) Bassett Hotel/McElmurray's Boarding House (Wilson's Gallery's building on East Church), and (3) 'Lubetkin House' (Fred's Discount Store). Directly across Jailhouse Alley from Lubetkin's was the Coca Cola Plant.

Van Noys, Choo-Choo, and Insurance Agencies

During the 1920s, the first floor of the Railroad Switching Tower became Van Noy's short order café. After WW II, during the late 1940s and early 1950s, Robert Tharpe established an ice cream parlor and eatery in the Switching Tower called the "Choo-Choo" where Fort Valleyans raved about the famous Frosted Malts. The establishment also served up delicious hamburgers and had pinball machines to entertain the youth. It was a favorite community dining and gathering place. After the railroad closed its passenger line during the late 1960s, the Passenger Station was sold. Shepard's Insurance Agency moved there and later Mayo Lacey's Valley Insurance Company. The palm trees in front of railroad complex have been there since the 1920s or earlier.

Fred Shepard recalls early years

Fred Shepard (whose grandfather was J. L. Fincher, Fort Valley mayor, 1904-1910, for whom Fincher Park is named) coordinated steam engine excursions from Fort Valley to Atlanta during the 1960s. Shepard enjoyed a personal acquaintance with the Southern Railroad President, Mr. W. Graham Claytor, who later became Secretary of the Navy. Fred tells the story of Mrs. Jennie Reid of Gaillard (six miles north of Fort Valley), who rode the first passenger train to Fort Valley in 1886.

"She was very patriotic and church-going; a nice lady," said Shepard. "She also ran a general store and post office at Gaillard." By 1964, Mrs. Reid had became too feeble to board the train, so Fred requested the Southern Railroad president to stop the train at Gaillard and pay tribute to her. President Claytor got off the train and presented a box of railroad drinking glasses to Mrs. Reid, sitting on her porch. "The newspapers carried the story," remarked Shepard.

Shepard also related that the old wooden passenger station caught on fire on April 15, 1906. "The townspeople had urged the railroad to tear down the dilapidated structure," said Shepard. "When the fire department started putting out the fire, the water hoses began spurting water." "Local citizens had cut the water hoses," laughed

Fred Shepard reminisces about early years of the railroad.

Shepard. "They wanted the structure to burn down!"

It was replaced with a brick passenger station and a switching tower/telegraph office around 1907. In 1924, a 430-feet shelter extended from the passenger station to the tower. The tower housed a restaurant on the ground floor and the telegraph office above.

Other remembrances

Spending the night on occasion at my Grandmother Braswell's house on Camellia Boulevard in Fort Valley during the early to mid-1940s, I would hear the whistles of trains passing through Fort Valley during the night. During my wife, Beverly's, first quarter at Shorter College in Rome, Georgia, in 1955, she rode the train from Fort Valley to Atlanta, changed trains in Atlanta, and proceeded on to Rome. My father, Lee Powell, a railroad enthusiast, loved to race his car along the highway with the trains speeding down the tracks, as my cousins Braswell Mathews and David Sammons will attest.

Railroad mergers; Today's Norfolk Southern

In 1869, the Southwestern Railroad leased its lines to the Central of Georgia Railroad, and by 1954 "the Central" absorbed the Southwestern Railroad. In 1963, the Southern Railroad purchased the Central of Georgia. In 1982, the Southern Railroad and Norfolk & Western Railroad merged and became the Norfolk Southern that operates through Fort Valley today.

Norfolk Southern train passes by old switching tower (L) and passenger station (R).

Old Freight Depot and Switching Tower to be restored

The Fort Valley Downtown Development Authority has obtained a $500,000 Department of Transportation grant to renovate the old Central of Georgia freight depot and create a museum. The museum will feature exhibits and memorabilia on three major entities in Fort Valley's storied past: the railroad, the peach industry, and Blue Bird Body Company. Renovation is scheduled to begin by early 2008. Once completed, the museum will generate increased tourism to Fort Valley and help revitalize the downtown area.

Plans are also in process to restore the old switching tower and to lease the ground floor to a business enterprise. The upstairs portion of the building will be restored to show the workings of a railway interlocking tower. This building is one of only a handful of structures of this type remaining in the country. The building that once housed the old passenger station is owned by Steve and Renee Caira. The popular Railroad Café operates out of this building. Preservation of the old railroad complex is encouraging. It will allow future generations of Peach Countians the opportunity to enjoy and appreciate our rich railroad heritage.

Sources: *History of Peach County Georgia*
Peach County, the World's Peach Paradise
   by Marilyn Neisler Windham
The Courthouse and the Depot by Wilber W. Caldwell
A Land So Dedicated by Bobbe Hickson Nelson
Fort Valley Downtown Development Authority
Selected articles from Internet

Chapter 4
Look at the pretty Blue Bird:
the early years of Blue Bird

Blue Bird Number 1

When Laurence Luce owned two Ford companies, one in Fort Valley and one in Perry, he never expected he would become one of the nation's premier manufacturers of school buses. His career path was radically changed in 1925 when the Penn-Dixie Cement Plant south of Perry ordered a bus to transport its workers. Luce procured the bus from a company in North Carolina and supplied it to Penn-Dixie. There was one rub, however. The bus, made with a wooden body, began to rot before it could be paid off. When the buyer from Penn-Dixie complained that the bus was poorly built, Luce agreed and remarked off the cuff, "I believe I can build a better bus than that myself." The buyer responded, "Why don't you?" That seed thought changed the course of Laurence Luce's career. Laurence figured that the problem posed by the wooden bus bodies was prevalent nation-wide and that the obvious solution was to build a metal bus.

By using mechanics from his Perry Ford company and the Fort Valley blacksmith, he began construction of a bus body. For the frame, he used angle iron to form a roof – a bow running from the floor to the roof. Sheets of steel fastened thereto comprised the body. Laurence's first bus was sold in 1927 to Frank Slade of Marshallville who used it to

Laurence Luce and Frank Slade with Blue Bird Number 1 in 1927.

haul school children. It was providential that Laurence's first bus became a school bus and not one to haul cement workers. Laurence produced his second bus in 1929 and his third in 1930.

The Turning Point

When the Depression hit, Laurence sold his Fort Valley Ford agency in 1930. This proved to be a wise decision, for auto sales at his Perry agency declined precipitously the following year: from 150 in 1930 to only ten in 1931. To keep his Perry enterprise, Houston County Motor Company, marginally solvent, he ramped up bus production and sales to a total of seven in 1931. Sensing a continuing economic slowdown, Luce faced a crisis. Either he could remain in the car business in Perry or sell it and devote his full energies to manufacturing buses.

One day Laurence's wife, Helen, approached him with inspiring advice. She said, "Laurence, the Lord has given you unusual abilities. I believe He has given you the ability to organize and manage a manufacturing plant." She reasoned that the trend toward bigger consolidated schools and better roads would increase the need to bus children to school. Consequently, Laurence sold his Perry Ford agency in 1932. That same year bus sales had climbed to twenty-five.

Helen Luce

Blue Bird Name

Laurence needed a business name to sell buses. "Blue Bird" was chosen after a salesman took a 'blue' demonstrator bus to a South Georgia school. When the school children saw the bus coming, they shouted, "Here comes the pretty Blue Bird."

From Peach Packing Shed to Livery Stable to New Plant

Laurence built buses in a rented peach packing shed on the Perry highway during 1933-34 and then moved his operation to a livery stable (site of Peach MAC) in Fort Valley. By the fall of 1935 construction of the new plant–near Five Points on Highway 49–was completed and Blue Bird moved in. Bus production picked up during the ensuing decade and profitability was evident.

Packing Shed – First Plant

Livery Stable – Second Plant

23

Fire Destroys Plant

On a cold wintry day in 1945, a coal burning stove caught the ceiling of the engineering room on fire. Quickly the flames engulfed the entire front of the plant. Laurence shouted, "Call the fire department" then ran upstairs with a fire extinguisher. In fighting the fire, he was overcome with smoke and collapsed. Jolly Bryant fearlessly went into the burning building, found Luce, and brought him to safety. "Jolly saved dad's life," said George Luce. A number of bus bodies were burned along with expensive equipment and machinery. Johnny Wells and his crews salvaged as much equipment as possible. The pacing factor in rebuilding the plant was a shortage of steel. Johnny Wells located 175,000 pounds of Junior T's in Knoxville, Tennessee, for sale. When welded together, the Junior T's formed the building's frame. For the roof and sides, galvanized metal sheets were purchased from the Tennessee Coal and Ice Company in Birmingham. While construction was underway, Blue Bird rigged a make-shift production line and continued making buses. Johnny Wells and J.E. Bozeman, the plant superintendent, helped rebuild the building and the company. Buster Beck, a longtime employee, said the first crews moved into the building during the early spring of 1946. "It was good to have everything back under one roof," remarked Beck. The fire was a blessing in disguise. Whereas Blue Bird's old building was inadequate and inexpansible, its new plant provided greater capacity and was readily expandable to accommodate future growth.

Heart Attack

It was October 1946. Walt Anderson noticed that Laurence Luce wasn't feeling well. Soon Walt heard attendants wheeling someone out the door to a waiting ambulance. He instinctively went to Helen Marshall, Luce's secretary, and asked who it was. "It's Mr. Luce," she said, her eyes filling with tears. "He's had a heart attack." Laurence was rushed to the hospital. For two weeks his life hung in the balance. When his doctors advised him not to remain actively engaged in the day-to-day operations of the company, his son, Albert L. Luce Jr. (Buddy) began serving as general manager of Blue Bird. For the next forty-four years, Buddy served in various capacities as general manager, president, and chairman of the board. From 1948 until 1953, George Luce and wife Willouise served as missionaries to the Belgian Congo,

Africa. George returned to Blue Bird in 1953. Laurence went to be with the Lord in 1962 and Miss Helen in 1976. From the day of their father's heart attack, the three Luce brothers—Buddy, George (except 1948-53), and Joseph (Joe)—were actively engaged in the management and operations of Blue Bird until it was sold to Merrill Lynch Capital Partners in 1992. Henlys purchased Blue Bird in 2001. The present owner is a bank syndicate called Peach County Holdings Inc. that took over plant operations in August 2005.

Laurence, George, Buddy, and Joe Luce

Blue Bird Expansion

During the Luce era, Blue Bird expanded its operations to every state in the Union, to every province in Canada, throughout Central America, and to other countries of the world. There were six plants in addition to the Fort Valley headquarters: Blue Bird Wanderlodge, Canadian Blue Bird, Blue Bird Midwest, Blue Bird East, Blue Bird Quebec, and Blue Bird Centro Americana.

Vignettes

Painted Car: Helen Luce drove in the yard one day with her friend, Wilma Orr. She was horrified to see that George, age four, and Buddy, three, had smeared white paint all over their black Ford automobile. The boys intended no harm. They just didn't like black and wanted to make it another color. They preferred to paint it orange, blue, or yellow, but white was the only color paint they could find.

Nut and Bolts: George and Buddy's first job was picking up bolts, nuts, and screws the workers had dropped. Their friend, Robert Braswell Mathews (renowned architect who resides in California), would help them. "Mr. Luce paid us eight cents an hour," said Mathews. "The bolts, nuts, and screws would be cleaned up and placed back into the bins for reuse."

Red Willie: Red Willie was the number one salesman selling aluminum pots and pans for the Aluminum Co. of America. He put on a demonstration at the home of A.L. Luce, and Laurence Luce and Buddy Luce bought twice as many pots and pans as they had intended. Mr. Luce wanted him to be selling school buses. He joined the Blue Bird firm and became the outstanding Blue Bird salesman in his territory.

Integrity Over Money: Orlando Rodriquez recalls a company manager in Havana, Cuba, wanting to buy one hundred and twenty buses. Money was not an issue. The sale was a done deal except the manager wanted Mr. Luce to add several hundred dollars to the cost of each bus as a kick-back to the manager. When Orlando translated this stipulation, Laurence canceled the sale.

Answered Prayer: Circa 1930-31. The stock market had collapsed and the economy had slipped into a deep depression. Making a payroll was difficult. Laurence's credit was over-extended at the bank yet he needed $500 to make payroll. The bank wouldn't let him have the loan. Laurence walked out on Main Street praying, "Lord, I am in a jam. Please help me."

Up the street came Robert L. Marchman Jr. (father of retired lawyer and Harvard graduate Bob Marchman). "What's wrong Laurence?"

"I'm in a tight bind. I have a payroll to meet this afternoon and the bank just turned me down."

"How much do you need?"

"Five hundred dollars...and I only need it for a week."

"That's no problem," said Marchman. "I'll give you my check and you give me yours." God answered the prayer through Marchman.

Source: *Wings of Blue Bird* by Bernard Palmer.

Chapter 5
Birth of a University:
History of Fort Valley State University

Events Leading to Creation of Fort Valley State College

Fort Valley State College (FVSC) and Henry Alexander Hunt High School shared a common origin (Reference *Leader Tribune* article, Sept. 1, 2004, "History of H. A. Hunt High School"). The chronology of events leading up to the creation of the college:

- 1895-Fort Valley High and Industrial School (FVHIS) began in Odd Fellows Lodge Hall.
- 1928-FVHIS gained junior college status.
- 1932-FVHIS became Fort Valley Normal and Industrial School (FVNIS).
- 1939- FVNIS merged with Teachers and Agricultural College of Forsyth and re-designated Fort Valley State College (FVSC). Academically separated were grades 1-7 (located in Peach County Training Building) and high school (housed in Peabody Trades Building: 1939-1944, and barracks beside St. Luke's Church: 1944-1954).
- 1941- High school named Henry Alexander Hunt High School after FVHIS's second principal.
- 1949-FVSC designated Georgia's land grant institution (state supported school for Negroes, teaching agriculture and mechanical arts) by the Georgia Legislature.
- 1954-Hunt High School and elementary grades 1-7 moved to new school constructed on Spruce Street.
- 1996-FVSC elevated to university status as Fort Valley State University (FVSU).

Fort Valley High and Industrial School

On November 6, 1895, eighteen men petitioned the Houston County Superior Court for a legal charter to start a school for blacks in Fort Valley. On January 6, 1896, the Houston Superior Court granted the petition and Fort Valley High and Industrial School (FVHIS) was incorporated. Its

Fort Valley State University had its humble beginnings at the Odd Fellows Lodge Hall located on O'Neal Street in Fort Valley.

eighteen petitioners–enshrined as school's founders on a plaque at the Hunt gravesite on FVSU campus–became the Board of Trustees. The FVHIS began in the Odd Fellows Lodge Hall located on O'Neal Street across from Usher's Temple Church. The school's first principal was John Wesley Davison (1862-1922). The school taught industrial arts and produced teachers for rural schools. Initial enrollment was 75 students. In 1896, four acres of land (around St. Luke's Episcopal Church) were purchased from Francis Gano and a three-story wooden building constructed. A third building was constructed in 1902. By the late 1890s, the school's enrollment had grown to approximately two hundred fifty students.

During 1903, Principal Davison resigned under pressure from the trustees, a dispute primarily over his curriculum being too academic and not sufficiently industrial. His successor was Henry Alexander Hunt (1866 -1938) who had graduated from Atlanta University with honors and had shown great promise as an educator. When Hunt and his wife, Florence Johnson Hunt, arrived in 1904 they found a small campus with only five buildings.

Soon after 1904 the FVHIS changed from an "ungraded" to a "graded" institution. Hunt believed that students should be taught skills (agriculture, carpentry, brick-laying, cooking, sewing, etc.) essential to making a livelihood. Henry A. Hunt's motto was "loyalty, thoroughness, and integrity." In 1931, Hunt was awarded the prestigious Spingarn Medal by the NAACP for devoted service to the education of blacks in rural Georgia.

The Fort Valley Normal and Industrial School

In 1928 the school gained junior college status, and in 1932 was renamed the Fort Valley Normal and Industrial School (FVNIS). Hunt served as FVHIS principal from 1904-1932, and FVNIS principal: 1932-1938. Student enrollment increased from 145 pupils in 1904 to over 1000 students in 1938, of which 103 were pursuing a junior college curriculum.

Creation of Fort Valley State College

Due to lingering financial constraints, Principal Hunt repeatedly attempted to obtain state support. He felt the time was ripe for Georgia to take over the Fort Valley school and to designate it as the state agricultural college; consequently, on March 20, 1938, the FVNIS trustees voted to transfer the institution to the State Board of Regents. Seven months later, Hunt passed this life on

October 1, 1938, but not before he saw his dream coming true—the school he had shepherded since 1904 was poised to become a full-fledged college.

In 1939, the regents merged the Teachers and Agricultural College of Forsyth with FVNIS, making it a four year institution and renaming it Fort Valley State College (FVSC). The following is a brief history of the Teachers and Agricultural College of Forsyth: (1) founded by William Merida Hubbard in 1900 with only seven students, (2) became a senior high school in 1916, (3) named the Agriculture and Mechanical School by the Georgia legislature in 1922, (4) renamed the Teachers and Agricultural College in 1931.

When the state assumed control of FVSC in 1939, its twenty-one-year affiliation with the national Episcopal Church ended. For two decades the national Episcopal Church provided funding under the terms that it maintain legal control of the college through a majority representation on its Board of Trustees. As a condition for relinquishing control, the national Episcopal Church requested and was paid $40,000 by the Julius Rosenwald Foundation. As part of the agreement, the Episcopal Church was granted acreage for a local church.

Ham and Egg Show

The annual Ham and Egg Show was originated by Otis Samuel O'Neal, the second black county agent. The first exhibition was held at the FVHIS auditorium in 1916. Local farmers competitively merchandized their farm products and received prizes awarded by judges. Its purpose was to encourage small farmers to produce more food for their families and for sale in the marketplace. The "show" was discontinued in 1969, when Robert Church was county agent, and replaced with the annual Ham and Egg Breakfast.

Succession of College Presidents

(1) Dr. Horace Mann Bond: 1939-1945 (2) Dr. Cornelius V. Troup: 1945-1966 (3) Dr. W.W. E. Blanchett: 1966-1973 (4) Dr. C. W. Pettigrew: 1973-died June 1982 (5) Dr. Walter W. Sullivan, acting President: 1982-1983 (6) Dr. Luther Burse: 1983-1988 (7) Dr. Melvin Walker Jr., acting President: 1988-1990 (8) Dr. Oscar Prater: 1990-2001 (9) Dr. Kofi Lomotey: 2001- 2005 (10) Dr. William Harris, acting President: July 2005-Mar 2006 (11) Dr. Larry Rivers: March 2006 to present.

Historical Tour of FVSU Campus

FVSU is steeped in history, a place where townspeople and visitors alike can relive the genesis and progression of this great institution. Start with the Anderson Building where guided tours are provided daily. This house, named after Benjamin S. Anderson, agriculture professor, was built for Francis W. Gano in late 1890s. It served as the home of FVHIS principal Henry A. Hunt and FVSC presidents Horace Bond and Cornelius Troup.

FVSC was largely Henry Alexander Hunt's creation. Hunt and his wife, Florence Johnson Hunt are entombed in front of Carnegie Hall. Fronting their graves is a plaque listing the eighteen original founders of the school in 1895.

Graves of Henry A. Hunt and Florence Johnson Hunt are enshrined on FVSU campus.

Jeanes Hall, erected 1904, was named after philanthropist Anna T. Jeanes. In 1907, Ms. Jeanes established a one million dollar foundation to support the ten black rural schools in the county. Those who oversaw the rural schools were called Jeanes supervisors. One such supervisor was Marion Bryant, wife of Henry Bryant, the beloved principal of Hunt High School from 1942-1970.

Huntington Hall, a girl's dormitory built in 1907, was constructed with a $25,000 contribution by Mrs. Collis P. Huntington, widow of a railroad financier. **The Peabody Trades Building**, 1926, was funded by Mrs. Royal Peabody in memory of her husband. High school students were schooled there until 1944 when it was damaged by fire. The Academic Building, 1929, was renamed **Founders Hall** in 1976 as a tribute to the institution's founders. The **John W. Davison Hall**, 1948, was named after the first principal of FVHIS. The **Henry Alexander Hunt Memorial Library** was dedicated 1952.

The **Alva Tabor Agriculture Building**, 1954, was named after Alva Tabor, a beloved teacher who established Negro FFAs and helped develop Camp John Hope. The **Cozy L. Ellison Agricultural Building**, 1965, was named after Ellison, first chairman of the Agriculture Department. William S. M. Banks was employed in 1940 as the first instructor of agriculture. **Myers Hall**, 1965, was a memorial to Henrietta Walden Myers, teacher of arts and crafts at FVNIS.

St. Luke's Episcopal Church has been the university church since 1939. The **Evans Building**, 1910, in downtown Fort Valley, was purchased by the college in 2001.

On Spruce Street is (1) **former Hunt High School**, (2) **plaque detailing its origin**, (3) **bronze bust of Henry E. Bryant**, (4) **time capsule** containing Hunt memorabilia to be opened in 2053, and (5) **Hunt Educational and Cultural Center** managed by Mrs. Evelyn McCray and its members. On O'Neal Street is a marker designating the site of **Odd Fellows Lodge Hall**.

FVSU Icons, L-R: Dr. Clinton Dixon, Dr. Isaac Crumbly, and Dr. Melvin Walker Jr. with a collective 115 years service to the university.

Dr. Donnie Bellamy, former history department chair, wrote highly acclaimed book about FVSU entitled Light in the Valley.

Fort Valley State University today

FVSU is part of Georgia's University System. Its 1,369 acres and thirty-five buildings comprise the state's second largest campus.

Bachelor's degrees are offered in thirty-seven majors, and master's degrees in education, animal science, public health, and counseling. Special academic programs are: Cooperative

Development Energy Program, Hospitality and Hotel Management, Commercial Design, Liberal Studies, and African World Studies. The high number of students accepted to medical colleges attests to strong programs in biology, chemistry, and veterinary technology. FVSU's 2600 students represent 130 of Georgia's 159 counties, thirty states and ten international countries. One-third of students live on campus. Off-campus sites are located in Macon, Warner Robins, Cochran, Dublin, and Vienna.

FVSU's Cooperative Extension Program serves forty-two counties. The Pettigrew Conference Center hosts five hundred courses and 51,000 patrons annually. Recent initiatives include the John W. Davison Lecture series and the African World Film Festival.

At right is Coach L. J. Lomax, famous football coach at FVSC. He was elected to the Georgia Sports Hall of Fame in 1996. His teams won four SIAC titles and advanced to NCAA playoffs twice. He produced a phenomenal 72 percent winning percentage. At left is Rev. Winfred Hope, former player and keynote speaker at Founder's Day.

FVSU is a member of the Southern Intercollegiate Athletic Conference (SIAC) and fields outstanding NCAA Division II teams in men's and women's sports.

FVSU, an esteemed institution with a rich heritage, has been an integral and vital part of the Fort Valley community for over a century. It is poised for future growth and continuing academic excellence.

Fort Valley State University: President, Department Heads, and Administrative Staff. First row, L-R: Dr. Judy L. Carter, Dr. Larry E. Rivers, President, Mrs. Gwendolyn D. Reeves, Dr. Daniel K. Wims. Second row: Dr. Melody Carter, Mr. Freddie L. Johnson, Dr. Kenneth Chatman. Third row: Mrs. Leslie Harriell-Turner, Mr. Donald Shavers, Mr. Katey Assem, Dr. Canter Brown Jr. Top row: Dr. Isaac J. Crumbly, Mr. Gregory D. Sills, Dr. Seyoum Gelaye, Mr. Wallace W. Keese.

Chapter 6
Henry Alexander Hunt's Dream: History of Henry Alexander Hunt High School

Fort Valley High and Industrial School (1895-1904)

Prior to the Civil War (1861-1865), formalized education for blacks in Peach County was non-existent. After the war and during reconstruction, concerted efforts were made to address the educational plight of blacks; as a result, the Fort Valley High and Industrial School (FVHIS) was organized in 1895.

On November 6, 1895, eighteen men petitioned the Houston County Superior Court for a legal charter. This petition in essence requested the court's approval to organize a school to promote the higher mental (academic) and manual (trade skills) education of its students. It further asked that the school be allowed to manage its own affairs, including hiring of teachers and selection of curriculum.

Three of the petitioners were white men: Francis Gano and local peach grower John Hale, both northerners; and Stephen Bassett, a Methodist minister. Three of the fifteen black petitioners were local pastors: Allen Cooper, Saint Peter AME; Peter Fann, Shiloh Baptist Church; and Lee O'Neal, Usher's Temple. The school's first principal was John Wesley Davison (1862-1922).

On January 6, 1896, the Houston Superior Court granted the petition and FVHIS was incorporated. Its eighteen petitioners—enshrined as the school's founders on a plaque at the Hunt gravesite on the FVSU campus—became the Board of Trustees. The FVHIS—a boarding school—began in the Odd Fellows Lodge Hall located on O'Neal Street across from Usher's Temple Church. In 1895, the lodge hall was serving as a school and a church. Usher's Temple, destroyed by fire in 1891, held its services there.

Principal Davison and his wife, Hattie, were FVHIS's first teachers. Enrollment was seventy-five students. The school taught industrial arts and produced teachers for rural schools. The school encountered financial problems and largely depended upon contributions from local citizens. In 1896, four acres of land were acquired (around St. Luke's Episcopal Church) and a two-story wooden building constructed. A third building was constructed in 1902. By the late 1890s, the school's enrollment approximated two hundred fifty students.

The Henry A. Hunt Years: 1904-1938

During 1903, Principal Davison resigned under pressure from the trustees, a dispute primarily over his curriculum being too academic and not sufficiently industrial. His successor was Henry Alexander Hunt Sr. (1866 -1938) who had graduated from Atlanta University with honors and had shown great promise as an educator. When Hunt and his wife, Florence Johnson Hunt, arrived in 1904, they found a barren campus with four buildings and one building under construction.

Soon after 1904, the FVHIS changed from an "ungraded" to a "graded" institution. Hunt believed that students should be taught skills (agriculture, carpentry, brick-laying, cooking, sewing, dress-making, basketry, etc) essential to making a livelihood. Henry A. Hunt's motto was "loyalty, thoroughness, and integrity" which characterized his career as an educator and the caliber of the students he produced. In 1931, Hunt was awarded the prestigious Spingarn Medal by the NAACP for devoted service to the education of blacks in rural Georgia.

In 1928, the school gained junior college status, and in 1932 was renamed the Fort Valley Normal and Industrial School (FVNIS). Hunt served as FVHIS principal from 1904-1932, and FVNIS: 1932-1938. Student enrollment increased from 145 pupils in 1904 to over one thousand students in 1938, of which 103 were pursuing a junior college curriculum.

The growth and expansion of the school was attributed to the untiring efforts of Henry Hunt and his wife, Florence, to secure financial support. Mrs. Collis P. Huntington, widow of a railroad financier, contributed $25,000 for a girl's dormitory in 1907. In 1916, the state's General Education Fund assisted in remodeling Jeanes Hall, and during the same year, Mrs. Royal C. Peabody provided funds to erect the Trades Building which bore her husband's name. The Carnegie Foundation added the Carnegie Library in 1925.

In addition to FVNIS, there were ten small rural black schools in the county: Little Bethel, Live Oak, Mathews, Myrtle, Oak Grove, Powersville, Red Level, Smyrna, Vinson, and Allen's Chapel in Byron. In 1907, philanthropist Anna T. Jeanes established a $1 million dollar foundation, bearing her name, to help these rural schools. In 1956, Superintendent Ernest Anderson consolidated these rural schools with the local school system and provided bus transportation.

Creation of Fort Valley State College (1939)

Due to financial constraints, Principal Hunt repeatedly attempted to obtain state support. He felt the time was ripe for Georgia to take over the Fort Valley school as the state agricultural college; consequently, on March 20, 1938, the FVNIS trustees voted to transfer the institution to the State Board of Regents. In 1939, the regents merged the Teachers and Agricultural College of Forsyth with FVNIS, making it a four year institution and renaming it Fort Valley State College (FVSC). The college's first president was Horace Mann Bond, from 1939-1945.

Formation of H.A. Hunt High School

Once FVSC was established in 1939, the high school and elementary grades were separated from the college. During the transition period, 1939-1940, an interim Fort Valley Laboratory School was established on the FVSC campus. Dr. C.V. Troup was its principal.

High school students (grades 8-11) remained on campus in the Peabody Trades Building. Those taking home economics and shop were schooled at the trade school building adjacent to the Peach County Training School on State College Drive.

In 1941, the high school was named H.A. Hunt High School after FVHIS's second principal, Henry Alexander Hunt Sr., who died in 1938. At the time of Hunt's death the Fort Valley High and Industrial School had thirteen modern buildings.

Florence Johnson Hunt died in 1953. She was a great lady and an important link between the school and the community. In 1934, a new infirmary on campus was named in her honor. Hunt and his wife, Florence, are buried on the campus near the Carnegie Building.

In 1944, the Peabody Trades Building was damaged by fire; consequently, the high school students were placed in barracks positioned between the Peach County Training School and St. Luke's Episcopal Church. There they stayed for the next ten years.

The elementary school (grades 1-7) remained in the Peach County Training School. The training school was erected in 1927 by the Julius Rosenwald Foundation, later torn down, and rebuilt in 1963 as the Gano building. It later became the college ROTC building and now houses a Pre-K program.

The first principal of H.A. Hunt High School was Aaron Brown. The second was Frank Davis. The third was Henry E.

Bryant, who served as principal from 1942 to 1970. Professor Bryant and his wife, Marion, were hired by Henry Hunt in 1935. Professor Bryant initially served as vocational agriculture teacher at FVNIS. Marion Bryant was a Jeanes Foundation supervisor with oversight responsibilities over the black rural schools. Jeanes Foundation supervisors included Annie R. Reed and Louise I. Batts.

Henry A. Hunt	*Florence Johnson Hunt*	*Henry E. Bryant,*
(1866-1938)	*(1866-1953)*	*Hunt High Principal,*
		1942-1970

Construction of New Schools on Spruce Street

Two new schools, H.A. Hunt High School (constructed by Board of Regents) and the Peach County Elementary School (built by Peach Board of Education), were ready for occupancy by 1954; consequently, the high school students (from barracks) and elementary grades (from the former Peach County Training Building) were moved to the Spruce Street location. A new and modern school for both high school and elementary school students was a long term dream of Henry A. Hunt, but he died sixteen years before it achieved fruition. Surely, he knew that one day his thirty-five-year pilgrimage to better the educational opportunities for blacks would be rewarded. It is so fitting that the high school was named after him. These facilities remained black schools until school desegregation in 1970. Today the old high school is occupied by the Department of Family and Children's Services.

School Integration

In 1970, the black and white schools in the county were integrated by federal court order. Ernest Anderson, superintendent of schools (succeeded J. F. Lambert in 1945) reorganized the school system into seven schools: one high school, one junior high and five elementary-primary schools. Total enrollment was 3,819 students: 1,399 white and 2,420 black.

H.E. Bryant Memorial and Time Capsule

Henry and Marion Bryant were among Fort Valley's most beloved citizens. To memorialize Professor Bryant's contributions to education and the community, a bronze bust in his likeness is prominently displayed in the courtyard of the old Hunt school complex. Nearby is a time capsule containing Hunt school memorabilia —sealed and buried on June 21, 2003, and to be opened in June 2053. Also on the grounds is an impressive plaque which details the origin, progress, and accomplishments of H.A. Hunt High School, whose cherished memory lives on in the hearts and minds of its graduates and supporters.

Hunt Educational and Cultural Center

In 1979, the Peach County BOE voted to tear down the dilapidated H.A. Hunt gymnasium. To preserve school heritage, Henry E. Bryant, Evelyn McCray, and others purchased the gym for $20,000 dollars. In 1980, the gym was co-founded by Mr. Bryant and Mrs. McCray as

Hunt Educational & Cultural Center (R) and former Hunt High School (L).

the Hunt Educational and Cultural Center. It was incorporated in 1981 and made a non-profit organization in 1994. Its mission is to preserve Hunt school history and to help meet the cultural, educational, social, and economic needs of the community.

Other charter members of the Hunt Educational and Cultural Center are Marion Bryant, Claybon Edwards, Mary Edwards Marshall, Rev. Julius Simmons, Anna L. Lumpkin, Gregory Homer, Otis Daniel, Norman Fitzgerald, James Latimore, Paulette McCray Neely, John Ezell Jr., Marie

Cleveland, Tollie Dodson, Darrell Fobbs, Gladys Grace, Ann Green, Eva Harris, Barbara Howard, Dorothy Jones, Haviland Nelson, Cecil and Betty Porter, and Cordie Walker.

Henry A. Hunt High School Graduates: front row L-R: Annie T. Jackson (graduated 1960), Mary Julia Edwards Marshall (1942), Mary Smith Brown (1968), Annette Snead Plant (1955), Betty Martin Porter (1961), Odessa Hardison McNair (1949), Carolyn H. Coleman (1946), Ruby H. Duffie (1950). Second Row: Jerry (Sim) Gibson (1952), Claybon J. Edwards (1945), Virginia M. Willis (1960), Elvira D. Culler (1956), Emma L. Aiken (1944), Dollie Dixon Horton (1959), Evelyn D. McCray (1948), Frances Hoskin (1943), Barbara Cousin Latimore (1964). Back row: Otis Lee Daniel Jr. (1972), Carolyn Watson Sampson (1947), Mamie Ruth Booth (1938), Cecil J. Porter (1956).

Sources: *Light in the Valley* by Dr. Donnie Bellamy
History of Peach County Georgia
Historical Notes of Evelyn McCray.

Chapter 7
Storied Past of Everett Square

Land Given by Everett and Dorsey: 1836

In 1836, James A. Everett (Fort Valley's founder) and business associate Mathew Dorsey gave six acres of land to the trustees of the Fort Valley male and female academies. The trustees were Hardy Hunter, Hugh Allen, James P. Allen, Henry Kaigler, James A. Everett, Allen Wiggins, John Humphries, William Harris, and A. M. Thompson. The land was deeded "in trust" with the stipulation that it be used forever for church and school purposes. This transaction was dated August 22, 1836, and recorded in the Houston County Superior Clerk's Office in Deed Book V, page 57. Before it became Everett Square, the tract was originally called "Beauty Square" for all the pretty girls who lived around the square. The first schools built on Everett Square were the Fort Valley Academy chartered in 1836 and the Wesley Manual Labor School for boys started in 1837.

The Old Pond Church (before moving to Everett Square)

The Fort Valley Methodist Church, organized in 1840, was first called the Old Pond Church. Historical records place the church one mile northwest of downtown Fort Valley and two miles from the Crawford County line. Soon after moving here in 1940, Bill Alford actually saw the remains of the Old Pond Church cemetery which adjoined the church. Bill said that one grave reflected the name Brigadier General Anderson, from the Revolutionary War. From his backyard, Bill pointed to the former church site: an area between the back of the School Bus Barn and the south end of Berkshire Drive. As late as fifteen years ago, Bill said a concrete pillar–about one foot square and eight feet tall–associated with the old church was still standing in that area. A pond is still there. In that

Dorothy Hudson (L), president of the Fort Valley Historical Society, and Marilyn Windham (R), Peach County historian, located the concrete pillar from the Old Pond Church in the wooded area behind the school bus barn.

same area, during the 1970s, Billy Marshall's sons, Johnny and David, found broken grave markers from the Old Pond Church cemetery. On one marker was etched the name "Wiggins." Billy said that Allen Wiggins, the school trustee mentioned above, was his great-great-grandfather.

Photos of the Old Pond Church are not available; however, historical records describe it as "an unpainted, wooden-frame building with a door at each end, shuttered windows, and wooden benches serving as pews." In those days the men sat on one side and the women on the other.

Old Pond Membership Moves to Everett Square: 1848

The Old Pond membership moved to Everett Square in 1848. The new building was erected near the point where Central Avenue dead-ends at Everett Square. The front of the church faced eastward toward Central Avenue. A balcony was added so slaves could attend services. Two aisles from the front led to the pulpit and altar area. This church was in a circuit with

The Old Pond Methodist membership built this church on Everett Square in 1848.

ten other churches. Its membership was forty-five males and fifty females. The former Old Pond church building was given to black worshipers. In 1866, this building was dismantled, carried across town by mule and wagon, and became Usher's Temple Church.

Church moves to corner of Church and Miller Streets: 1901

In April 1895, since additional space was needed to accommodate Sunday School, the Methodist Church appointed Judge H. A. Mathews (grandfather of Beth Mathews Collins and Mary Mathews Humble) as chairman of a building committee to explore the feasibility of erecting another church and raising $50,000 dollars for its construction. Members of the committee were Rev. O. A. Thrower, G. P. Green, J. M. Jones, W. C. Wright, F. O. Miller, J. L. Fincher, W. D. Sandwich, and S. B. Brown Jr.

At a quarterly church conference during 1900, the proposal was made to buy land on the corner of Church and Miller Streets to construct a new church. The lot, called the Simpson lot, extended one hundred feet along Church Street and two hundred feet down

Miller Street. After several motions and counter-motions, a roll-call vote was taken. T. G. Shepard called the roll and J. L. Fincher tallied the votes. The result was seventy-five for accepting the Simpson lot and fifty-four for staying at the present site. Several members expressed opposition and one member requested his name be stricken from the church register. The land was deeded to the church on September 15, 1900.

Despite significant divisions in the church, the new brick structure was dedicated in 1901 and work completed in 1902. This is essentially the same church we see today except for three subsequent additions: Sunday School Annex, 1918; Fellowship Hall and Chapel, 1954; and Educational Building built in 1967 on a lot donated by Dr. V. L. Brown Jr.

Grady Institute: 1886-1911

As early as 1886, Fort Valley had a public school system. The Grady Institute, named after Henry W. Grady, editor of the *Atlanta Constitution* during the 1880s, consisted of four rooms with a stage. It was located on the corner of College and Miller Streets, where the Evans-

The Grady Institute during the late 1890s.

Cantrell House sits today. Completing nine grades was required for graduation. In 1895, one hundred pupils were enrolled in the school. The best known and most beloved principal of the school was Professor W. J. Scroggs, who lived on Everett Square in a house later occupied by the J. E. Davidsons.

Public School System Moves to Everett Square: 1912

In 1912, the Grady Institute was replaced by a new two-story, brick building built on Everett Square. It was designed by Professor Scroggs's son Phil, an architect. Ralph Newton, a graduate of Mercer University, was the first principal. The new school housed grades one through eleven.

In 1920, due to overcrowding, grades 1-4 were moved to two clapboard buildings (both two story) near the west end of College Street, in proximity to the present Valley Cable TV office. Fred

The Fort Valley school building constructed at Everett Square in 1912.

Shepard, Marcus Hickson Jr., Wallis Hardeman, Judge George Culpepper, George Luce, Henry Outler, Muriel Halprin Nathan, Margaret Baldwin and Helen Harris attended primary school there. Grades 5-11 remained at Everett Square.

High School Moves to Knoxville Street: 1927

The Peach County School System came into being on January 1, 1925, following the creation of Peach County by the State Legislature on July 18, 1924. Ralph Newton was its first superintendent and served until 1928.

Fort Valley High School built in 1927.

The public school outgrew the building on Everett Square; consequently, a new high school was built in 1927 on Knoxville Street. With grades 6-11 moving to the Knoxville Street location, the Everett Square school retained grades 1-5.

J. F. Lambert served as superintendent from 1928 until 1945. Ernest R. Anderson became the third superintendent in 1945 and served forty years, until the end of 1984.

In 1952, the two-story Everett Square school was torn down–due to disrepair and a badly leaking roof—and a one-story primary school (grades 1-3) constructed.

The primary school on Everett Square was vacated when school integration occurred in 1970. It housed county offices for a number of years. On October 2, 1999, the dilapidated primary school was burned by the city fire department and later razed.

Everett Square Today

The City of Fort Valley now owns Everett Square. Seeing the need to develop Everett Square into a park for the enrichment of all citizens, the Fort Valley Downtown Development Authority chartered the Everett Square Park Committee to accomplish this objective. The committee, chaired by William Khoury, proposes the following additions to the park: (1) a veterans' memorial, (2) a plaza and amphitheater, (3) a bandstand, and (4) garden rooms. Paved walkways and lighting are planned. Funding will be raised primarily through donations and grants. American Legion Post 76 is seeking donations specifically for the veterans' memorial.

A hundred-year time capsule, entitled "The Way We Were," was buried at Everett Square in 1999 by the Peach County Historical Society and will be opened in 2099.

Chapter 8
The Murder and Haunting at Sleepy Hollow

Sensational stories, gossip, and speculation regarding the murder and haunting at the Sleepy Hollow Farm near Marshallville, Georgia, have been swirling for over seven decades. Tales of haunting began to surface in 1934 after a sensational shooting at the Sleepy Hollow lodge in which the farm overseer, E. Lynn Fagan, shot and killed farm owner George Slappey for allegedly making suggestive and improper advances toward Fagan's wife. The murder occurred on Friday morning, July 20, 1934. With the passing of years, the old lodge became the most famous haunted house in the area.

During my teen years, my mother's cousin, Charlie Gray of Fort Valley, Georgia, would regale me for hours with spine-tingling stories about the ghosts that roamed the abandoned lodge at Sleepy Hollow. The two-story lodge, located barely over the Peach County line in Macon County, was built in the late 1920s by the flamboyant George Slappey (1871-1934), a wealthy peach grower. Cousin Charlie told of hearing a person sobbing upstairs, of blood-curdling screams that would shatter the silence of night, of an

Farm owner Kemper Hunnicutt stands in front of the ominous black pond where mysterious deaths have occurred.

unseen presence felt on the staircase, and of doors and window shutters slamming for no apparent reason. He warned me of the creepy, ominous-looking pond of pitch-black water near the house. He stated that two farm hands had mysteriously drowned in the deep, dark pond—that an unseen hand would suddenly reach out of the water and drag an unsuspecting person to the bottom. Adding to the legend of the pond, George Hunnicutt, son of Kemper Hunnicutt and current owner of the old lodge site, stated that years ago a woman walking across a foot bridge at the pond, fell over backwards for no apparent reason, broke her neck and died. Feeling the place was both spooked and jinxed, no one since has wanted to go near the old pond. I, for one, would not dare linger at the edge of the pond, nor would I go there alone.

George Slappey's grandfather was George Hiley Slappey (1812-1886), who lived with his ten children in a two-story antebellum home in Marshallville— a showcase of the old South that has been renovated and is now owned by Jimbo Liipfert. The elder Slappey gave the Sleepy Hollow plantation to his oldest son, Jacob Class Slappey, who fought in the Civil War and fathered eight children. Jacob's son, George, built the lodge at Sleepy Hollow during the late 1920s with lumber taken from the boyhood home of George W. Mathews, a Methodist minister and grandfather of George, Buddy, and Joe Luce, former owners of Blue Bird Body Company in Fort Valley.

During the 1920s and through the mid-1930s, George Slappey operated the farm at Sleepy Hollow. His overseer was Lynn Fagan, who specialized in maintaining farm equipment. According to the *History of Peach County*, Slappey was a "farmer, fruit grower, and pharmacist (owned a drug store in downtown Fort Valley), interested in public affairs, and a constant 'writer to the editor.'" In 1917, he opened the Austin Theater in downtown Fort Valley where local citizens enjoyed stage plays for years. The theater was named after Slappey's friend, Samuel "Bully" Austin, who was the son of Dr. David N. Austin, and served as editor of the local newspaper named *The Leader*. After the creation of Peach County in 1924, the building that formerly housed the Austin Theater became the first county courthouse; its offices were located on the second floor. On the first floor was a reputable clothing store owned and operated by my great uncle, R. S. Braswell. During the late 1930s, the old Austin Theater building was converted to a movie theatre in the Martin-Thompson theater chain and was named the Peach Theater.

Buddy Luce, son of Albert Laurence Luce, who founded Blue Bird Body Company, remembers Slappey as a wealthy peach grower, who owned land between Fort Valley and Marshallville and operated a peach packing shed. Buddy tells the story of Slappey trying to cash a check in New York City. For verification, the New

York bank called the local bank. Buddy stated, "Mr. Martin, the bank president, told them to check Slappey's suspenders and if he has two buttons on each side of his pants, then cash his check."

Fred Shepard, who helped Buddy's father build his first school buses in a shed where Peach Maximum Auto Care in Fort Valley sits today, stated that he remembers going to Sleepy Hollow with his mother and his aunt, Mrs. Jenny Vance, to see Slappey's new lodge in the late 1920s. They knocked on the door and George Slappey invited them in. "The house was an elegant place with a ballroom for dancing and a staircase going up to the second floor," Fred observed. "There were two pianos for dancing, one for square dancing and the other for round dancing." While talking with Fred's mother and Mrs. Vance, Slappey remarked how much he enjoyed piano music and commented that he would like to have a piano rendition played at his funeral. On the way home, according to Fred, Mrs. Jenny Vance muttered under her breath, "Where George Slappey's going; there won't be any time for dancing."

Buddy Luce also revealed that Slappey once lived in the Hollingsworth home on Anderson Avenue across the street from the current post office and that he buried his beloved dog named 'Snowball' behind the house and covered the grave with a granite marker. The dog's grave is still in view near the fence behind the old Hollingsworth house. Fred Shepard related that, when Snowball died, Slappey remarked, "That was the saddest funeral in my life."

The grave marker of Slappey's beloved dog, Snowball, still resides behind the old Hollingsworth home.

Fred Shepard also disclosed that Slappey had a black chauffeur, Freddie Brookins of Marshallville, to drive him around in a Pierce-Arrow automobile, a luxury vehicle in those days. On one occasion Slappey had his chauffeur drive up alongside Shepard's family car on the way to Macon near Echeconnee Creek and tossed candy through the car window to little Fred sitting in the backseat of his parent's car.

George Slappey loved to party and would invite guests for the weekend. Some would stay overnight at the lodge. Wild drinking parties, dancing, and debauchery at Slappey's lodge started as early as Thursday evening and extended through the weekend. Celetta Grice, an 88-year old Marshallville native and Wesleyan graduate, recalled that weekend dances were held at Sleepy Hollow during the late 1920s and early 1930s. Celetta was a friend of Slappey's Aunt Hannah. Mrs. Grice described Slappey as "a distinguished-looking southern gentleman of large stature with a mustache and white hair." Mrs. Grice said Slappey was not married during the time she knew him—during the late 1920s until his death. In fact, Slappey's first wife, Fannie Harris (1873-1893), died during childbirth (child also died) two years after their marriage in 1891. Fannie was the daughter of H.C. Harris, owner of the old Winona Hotel. Slappey's second wife, Clara Visscher, reportedly a beautiful lady, died in 1919. According to Thomas Fleming Flournoy's *Early History of Fort Valley,* published in 1975, Clara, in a state of delirium before her death, admitted to sexual indiscretions, so Slappey never marked her grave. His third wife was Eva Kavannaugh. Slappey and Kavannaugh were not married after he built Sleepy Hollow Lodge during the late 1920s and held weekend dances there.

Footloose, fancy-free, and filthy rich, George Slappey evidently was drawn to pretty women, which was the case with the farm overseer's wife, the former Emily Keen, who was said to be an attractive woman. Emily's father, Will Keen, ran a country store and gas station owned by Slappey on the Marshallville highway, directly across Georgia Highway 49 from the present Camellia Gardens. Lynn Fagan married Emily Keen after his first wife died. They lived in the farm overseer's quarters, which comprised four rooms annexed on the north end of the Sleepy Hollow Lodge. Reportedly, Slappey spent a lot of time at the lodge and was very attentive to Emily every time he saw her. The story has been circulating for years that Slappey would follow Emily to town when she went to visit her parents who lived on Persons Street in Fort Valley. Their home is now owned by Calvin and Joyce Mason, who purchased the home from the Keen estate during the 1970s. According to an account told by Calvin Mason, Lynn Fagan was suspicious and followed Slappey to Fort Valley one day. There he caught Slappey at the front door of the Keen home talking to Emily through the screen door and trying to get in. When Slappey spotted Lynn Fagan rounding the corner onto Person's Street in his vehicle, he jumped in his automobile and sped back to Sleepy Hollow. Reportedly, Lynn Fagan warned Slappey never to bother his wife again. In Flournoy's history, the shooting was described this way: "For some reason Lynn (Fagan) thought George (Slappey) was getting too familiar with Emily. One night after George had come to the apartment (the Fagan's living quarters at the Sleepy Hollow Lodge) calling Emily, Lynn followed him to his room and shot him."

Hearing at Macon County Courthouse

A hearing was held before City Court Judge R.L. Greer on July 25, 1934, five days after the murder. After hearing the evidence, Judge Greer committed the case to the November 1934 session of the Macon County Grand Jury.

The July 26, 1934, issue of the *Macon County Citizen* reported the following testimony at the hearing:

"Lynn Fagan confessed slayer of George H. Slappey, for whom he acted as farm overseer, was committed to the Macon County Grand Jury on a charge of voluntary manslaughter Tuesday morning at a hearing before Judge R. L. Greer, of city court. Bond of $1500 was furnished and Fagan was released immediately after the hearing was concluded.

"A crowd of 500 taxed the capacity of the main court room of the Macon County courthouse and listened with rapt attention to the testimony, which was practically the same as that given at the coroner's inquest, a few hours after the killing, Friday morning (July 20).

"Fagan took the stand on his own behalf and reiterated his assertion at the inquest, that he did not intend to kill his employer, but that his pistol was discharged after he had struck Mr. Slappey on the head. The slayer said that the fatal argument with his employer was over alleged attentions to Mrs. Fagan, and that he struck Mr. Slappey on the head with his pistol only after his employer had reached for his gun on a nearby bed. 'He went for his pistol and I grabbed his arm,' Fagan told the court. 'I hit him with mine (gun), and the gun went off. I didn't mean to shoot him. Before God, I didn't mean to shoot him.' Fagan said he had been under a 'terrible strain for the past ten days.' He said that Mr. Slappey's undue attentions to his wife began a week ago last Sunday (July 15) and that Wednesday morning (July 18) his employer came to the Fagan's room, 'grabbed her and kissed her on the arm' The next afternoon (Thursday, July 19) 'he came in and caught her and kissed her on the cheek,' Fagan continued. 'She asked me to take her away, said she was afraid to stay there any longer, but I told her that we had no place to go.'

"Taking of the testimony required almost an hour, and in

less than another hour, at 4:45 p.m. (CST), Judge Greer rendered his decision (charged Fagan with voluntary manslaughter and committed case to the Grand Jury).

"During the hearing, Mrs. Fagan (the former Emily Keen) sat by her husband at the counsel table.

"Solicitor General Hollis Fort of Americus conducted the prosecution, and he was assisted by the Macon law firm of Smith and Smith and by Thomas Slappey, Atlanta attorney, who was a relative of the dead man.

"Fagan was exonerated at the coroner's inquest Friday (July 20), but was arrested on a murder warrant by Sterling Slappey, brother of the dead man, a short time later.

"Mr. Slappey made a fortune from the sale of peaches and at one time was the state's largest shipper. He was noted for his generosity and hospitality and gave many ... parties at Sleepy Hollow, which is just across the Macon County line from Peach County."

Grand Jury Indictment and Court Trial

The Grand Jury on November 12, 1934 issued a true bill, indicting Fagan for murder.

At the criminal trial that followed, Solicitor General Hollis Fort of Americus conducted the prosecution and was assisted by Smith and Smith law firm of Macon and Thomas Slappey, a relative of the dead man. Witnesses for the state were Dr. G. W. Nelson, Dr. D. B. Frederick, Freddie Brookins, and R.C. Souder. Attorneys George B. Culpepper Jr. (Judge George Culpepper's father) and Jule Felton defended Fagan.

Fagan was acquitted. On the back of the Grand Jury indictment, the criminal jury foreman, W. H. Ansley, wrote: "We the jury find the defendant not guilty," and dated the verdict "11-15-34." The not guilty verdict rendered by the criminal jury was predictable, as juries in those days had no tolerance for any man who attempted to violate another's wife. Macon County had no transcript of the actual court proceedings. In those days, unless there was a conviction, a trial record was not maintained.

The citizens of Peach and Macon Counties will never know what really happened at Sleepy Hollow. That's because the hearing produced the testimony of only one man directly involved in the shooting–Lynn Fagan. George Slappey was dead and could not represent his side of the story, and Fagan's wife was not put on the witness stand. According to Fagan's testimony, there was a scuffle in the bedroom prior to the shooting. Something had made Fagan mad enough to bring his gun along. Although no one can say with certainty what transpired, the shooting has been the subject of wild speculation fueled by vivid imaginations for decades.

George Slappey loved life and did not want to die. Only sixty-three years old when he was struck down, Slappey had a bright future ahead in business and many opportunities to reap greater rewards in life. Since his tenure on earth was cut short before he had a chance to realize his dreams, many believe his ghost continued to roam the lodge seeking fulfillment. Reports of the haunting at Sleepy Hollow were not isolated incidents, but were widespread occurrences over many years. Did his ghost depart the lodge when it was torn down? Well, I won't be caught in the dead of night standing inside the still-standing brick cellar of the lodge to find out.

Fort Valley's *Leader Tribune*, dated July 26, 1934, did not mention murder in Slappey's obituary, but called his passing on July 20, 1934 a "sudden death that shocked the community." A great uncle of this writer, R.S. Braswell, was a pallbearer. Other local pallbearers were Jerome Walker of Marshallville and W.D. Thorpe and C.M. Orr of Fort Valley. Slappey (1871-1934) was buried in Oaklawn Cemetery in the Harris lot beside his first wife, Fannie Harris Slappey (1873-1893). His grave is located one hundred feet directly north of the Confederate flagpole and is near a large cedar tree.

Graves of George Slappey and first wife, the former Fannie Harris, in Oaklawn Cemetery

Sleepy Hollow during the 1940s-1960s

Sleepy Hollow was a place frequented by young people during the 1940s, 1950s, and 1960s. Many believed it to be haunted and wanted to see a real ghost. For the sheer excitement, dating teenagers would frequent the area and park near the old lodge. Uninvited visitors coming to the abandoned house for thrills were a constant problem for Kemper Hunnicutt, who purchased the farm from the Slappey estate. Hunnicut worried that someone might be injured.

I distinctly recall going to Sleepy Hollow the night after my Perry High School basketball team had won the state championship in March 1953. There were three boys and three girls in the party. We arrived at the Sleepy Hollow Lodge about an hour before midnight. All six of us entered the dark lodge with a single flashlight and immediately went up stairs where the shooting occurred. I stayed near

Kemper Hunnicutt stands in front of the remains of the former haunted house that was torn down in 1968. George Slappey was shot to death inside the lodge in 1934.

the stairwell as the others went into the different upstairs rooms. As I listened to shrieks of apprehension and excitement from the girls, I distinctly felt a presence and a rush of cold air as if an unseen spirit had passed me going down the stairs. My hair literally stood on end. I wanted to get out of there, and quickly. I hollered to the group: "Let's get out of here; there's a ghost in this place!" A stampeded ensued and a young lady, in her haste, turned her ankle going down the stairs and fell. I vowed never to go there again. The mere thought of encountering a ghost in the darkness of the old abandoned lodge would send shivers down my spine.

Sleepy Hollow Today

Kemper Hunnicutt, a bomber pilot who flew sixty-five missions over Germany, rented the nine hundred-acre farm when he returned from the war in 1947. Hunnicutt purchased it in 1975 from R.C. Souder of Macon, who married Slappey's sister, Maude. Located two miles off highway 49 on Doles-Sleepy Hollow Road, which is south of Fort Valley and near the Peach-Macon County line, the lodge, which once hosted big dances on weekends, was torn down by Hunnicutt in 1968. All that remains of the old lodge are the basement foundation and a three-tiered brick chimney that heated the first and second floors of the lodge as well as its basement. Annexed to the lodge were four rooms—two upstairs and two downstairs-- where the overseer and his wife lived.

Is Sleepy Hollow still haunted? I don't know, but when I visited Kemper Hunnicutt at Sleepy Hollow, I particularly avoided venturing near the foreboding black pond. I caution all curiosity seekers to stay away from the old pond, especially when alone; sightseeing there could cost you your life.

Sources: *Early History of Fort Valley* by Thomas F. Flournoy
Macon County Georgian
Macon County Court records
The Leader Tribune
Interviews with local citizens

Chapter 9
The Axe Slaying and Mutilation on Possum Trot

Mutilated Body Found on Railroad Tracks

On Thursday, December 9, 1943, the nude and mutilated corpse of John Benjamin Jump, a 53-year old white man, was found lying on the Southern Railroad tracks near the Atlantic Ice and Coal Plant in Fort Valley. Ice was made there to refrigerate boxcars of peaches that would be transported to northern markets. An ice plant worker, hurrying to work around 5:30 a.m. while it was still dark, almost stumbled across the dismembered body.

Jump lived in the area that the old timers called "Possum Trot," which encompassed old Fairground Street (now Commercial Heights) and the connecting road leading east to the Cotton Mill. Possum Trot in those days represented the general area between the site of the current McDonald's restaurant and the railroad tracks to the east.

The authorities were called and shortly Peach County Sheriff Herbert Beeland, Fort Valley Police Chief Grady Cochran, and Town Constable W. T. Skellie were scurrying down the railroad tracks at Five Points, where five major roads converge at the north side of town, near Blue Bird Body Company.

Two sections of Jump's body, severed at the waist, were found lying across the railroad tracks: his upper torso including chest and arms lay separated from his lower body comprising hips and legs. His head, severed at the neck, was spotted in a ditch about twenty-five feet from his body. The position of the body parts indicated that Jump had been run over by a train. Historian Calvin Mason recalled that the Jumps lived

Police Chief Grady Cochran and Sheriff Herbert Beeland search the railroad tracks.

about where the Burger King stands today, and that Jump's body was found on the tracks that run behind the present Days Inn Motel. The body was found on the railroad tracks approximately 200 yards from the Jump home.

Killer picked a Ghost Train to cover up his crime

Arriving soon at the scene was Sergeant James Addy of the Georgia Bureau of Investigation, who began taking photographs and gathering evidence. Addy remarked, "These slashes are too clean for the man to have been killed by a train."

"I agree," Chief Cochran stated. "Everyone knows that trains haven't run on this rail spur for years."

Sheriff Beeland concluded, "This was meant to look like an accident."

Beeland added, "The killer made a big mistake. He picked a ghost train to cover up his crime."

The police chief, acknowledging that the townspeople knew the spur track was unused, opined, "This crime may have been committed by out-of-towners."

GBI investigator James Addy.

GBI investigator Addy noticed that Jump's severed head revealed a deep gash on the back of the scalp. "That blow probably killed him," he said. "Then one or more persons cut him up and brought him here." Also found was a long bloodstained splinter that could have caused the deep wound observed on the victim's calf. The splinter came from pine wood, indicating that Jump's dead body may have been dragged across a pine floor. Adding to the supposition that Jump had been killed elsewhere was the fact that little blood was present at the murder scene. Obviously, the body had been placed on the tracks to simulate an accident.

Tire marks were noted on a dirt road near the railroad tracks, prompting agent Addy to take pictures of the tread marks.

Constable Skellie stated that two weeks earlier, on November 27, Jump married a divorcee with two small children by her first husband.

Fort Valley's *Leader Tribune* on Thursday, December 9, 1943, published this front page story covering the murder:

"The stark body of a man identified as John Jump was found brutally hacked to death and still warm, on the Southern Railroad tracks in the vicinity of the Atlantic Ice and Coal Plant early this morning. The gruesome discovery was made about 6 o'clock by a Negro employee of the railroad who immediately summoned city and county policemen to the scene of the crime.

"It was definitely established that the murder did not take place on the spot where the body was found. *There was little blood and marks on the surrounding grass and dirt indicating that the dismembered body of the victim had been dragged for some distance and placed on the tracks in an effort to cover up the crime.* *The track was seldom used and no trains had passed over it recently.*

"While reluctant to disclose names prematurely, police officers report that there is little doubt that the murderer will be placed under arrest within a few hours.

"An employee of the cotton mill, Jump had lived in Fort Valley for the past two years. *Survivors include his widow and a daughter in Tifton, and one son who is in the army."*

Autopsy Report

After special agent James Addy completed his investigation, Coroner W. A. Williams drove up in an undertaker's wagon and transported the body to the medical laboratory in Macon, Georgia, where doctors labored through the night to perform a post mortem examination. The report disclosed that the skull had been split open with one cleaving blow of an axe and the dismemberment accomplished with a sharp knife. The autopsy revealed that Jump had been dead about twenty-four hours, placing the murder the previous day, Wednesday, December 8, about ten to eleven p.m.

Coroner W. A. Williams quickly assembled a coroner's jury that returned a verdict of murder by an unknown killer.

Officers Question Jump's Widow

The three investigators decided to talk to Jump's widow, Elise Jump, who was only twenty-two years old and had two small children by a previous marriage. When the trio arrived at the Jump home and spoke to Elise Jump, Addy said, "We have come to talk with you about your husband."

The woman's eyes widened. "What's happened to John?" she demanded. "He didn't come home last night. We've only been married since November the twenty-seventh."

"Suppose you tell us the circumstances of your husband's failure to come home," inquired Addy. Elise Jump stated that she and her husband worked at the Fort Valley Cotton Mill and that every work day they carried the children to a neighborhood babysitter before work at seven in the morning and picked them up after work around 7:00 p.m.

"We rode to work in our car," said Mrs. Jump. "We would come home together and pick up the children. Last night after work, I waited outside the mill in the car for John for about an hour, but he never showed up."

"So you came home alone and picked up the children from the babysitter?" inquired Addy.

"Yes, I picked up the kids," responded Mrs. Jump. She added, "I was very upset because John had never done that before, and I didn't go to work today because I thought John would come home."

When they broke the news that her husband had been murdered, she screamed and began sobbing. Once she regained her composure, Elise stated that her folks, who lived at a settlement several miles north of Fort Valley, didn't want her to marry Jump because of the age difference. She added that a young fellow in Fort Valley about her age, Sam Redding, had told her that she was crazy to marry Jump. "But, I needed a husband to make a home for my kids," she stated. Before leaving the premises, the three investigators inspected Jump's car. Finding the tires smooth, they ruled out her car, since the treads at the murder scene left a distinct imprint on the road.

Elise Jump

Full Scale Investigation Begins

A full-scale investigation ensued. Beeland and Addy drove to the settlement situated north of Fort Valley where the relatives of Mrs. Jump lived, to determine a possible motive for the murder. Meanwhile, Skellie checked at the cotton mill to determine when the Jumps were last seen together. Chief Cochran picked up for questioning Sam Redding, a former suitor of Mrs. Jump, who had been vocal about Jump's cruelty to his family and had speculated that the marriage would not last.

Beeland and Addy, after visiting with Elise Jump's kinfolk, learned that her relatives were regarded as solid citizens and not the type to harm anyone. Their primary concern regarding the marriage was the thirty-year age difference and had discouraged Elise from marrying Jump. Elise's relatives were not surprised when told of Jump's murder. They revealed that Jump did not make friends easily and had created some enemies.

Redding, when questioned, laughed at the suggestion he killed Jump. "Not me," he replied. "If Elise preferred him to me, that's okay. Sure I was sore about it for a while but that's all. But I'm wondering if Elise didn't have a good reason for knocking his block off. He treated her like a dog. I met her on the street one day and she told me Jump had beaten her on their wedding night." Redding had a perfect alibi. Since he was at a cockfight with friends eight miles outside town at the time of the murder, he was released. The investigators further reasoned that Redding, a local citizen, certainly would have known that the spur track was not used and would not have made the mistake of placing the body on the tracks.

Elise Jump's first husband also was ruled out as a suspect as he was five hundred miles away at the time of the slaying.

Break in the Case

Constable Skellie reported that cotton mill workers had seen Jump and his wife crossing the mill yard together after work on Wednesday, December 8, the night of the murder.

"Someone must have lured him away right after that," conjectured Skellie.

Addy, rubbing his chin, remarked, "We have overlooked a possible witness. What about the babysitter?"

They immediately headed to the babysitter's house. The babysitter acknowledged keeping the Jump's children and stated John Jump picked up the children on Wednesday night—the night he was murdered.

"Was Mrs. Jump with him?" Addy asked. The woman nodded 'yes.'

Realizing that Elise Jump had lied about her husband not coming home from work and not being with her when the children were picked up at the babysitter's house, the three officers began searching the field behind Jump's house. There they found marks of a body being dragged. The frost-covered field was soaked with blood. Near the house, they discovered an axe and a shotgun well hidden in the brush behind the house.

Killer's confession: "It was him or me."

When confronted again by the three law enforcement officers, Elise Jump confessed to the murder. "I knew you'd get back to me sooner or later," she said. "John was cruel, beating me and the children. He was planning to kill me. Right after supper Wednesday night he got drunk and threatened my life. He had

a shotgun and said he was going to blow my head off. I got the gun away from him and hid it outside. An hour later, it started again. He got an axe and said he was going to chop my head off. I talked to

Axe used by Elise Jump to kill husband.

him and got him to sit down in the kitchen rocker. He wasn't getting any calmer so I waited my chance. It was him or me. I finally got a chance to grab the axe. He was still in the chair, so I hit him over the head. He fell to the floor and I knew he was dead."

She continued, "I knew I had to get rid of the body and thought of the railroad tracks behind the house. I decided to cut him up and put his body on the tracks. I didn't know the trains

Sheriff Beeland and Police Chief Cochran search behind Jump house for clues.

weren't running on that track. I guess I also made a mistake in taking his clothes off. There was only fifty cents in his pocket. I used a carving knife from the kitchen drawer to cut him up. I put his clothes in the stove and started a hot fire. Then I dragged him across the field. Finally I felt safe."

The three officers found two buttons and a suspender clasp in the ash pit of the stove, indicating Jump's bloody clothes had been burned. The kitchen floor had been scrubbed, yet bloodstains were still visible between the planks. They also found a three-inch tear in the splintery pine floor that was made by dragging the body. This accounted for the bloody splinter found near the dismembered body and the deep gash it made in Jump's leg.

The *Leader Tribune,* dated December 16, 1943, reported Elise Jump's confession:

"Held without bail in the Bibb County jail, Mrs. Elise Jump is awaiting trial for the self-confessed murder of her husband, John Jump, whose mutilated body was discovered here last Thursday morning.

"The 22-year old bride of a few weeks calmly admitted that she knocked her husband out with an axe and then decapitated and bisected his body with a butcher knife after he made threats against her. She then carried the pieces to the railroad tracks, and returned to the house where she tried to remove all signs of the crime.

"Reported as being a model prisoner, the young mill worker is said to appear cheerful and giving no trouble. Her two children by a previous marriage are being cared for by friends. She is expected to go on trial in superior court at the January term."

After her arrest, Mrs. Jump was held in the jail in Macon, Georgia, because they had no provisions for a woman in the Peach County jail. On December 15, 1943, Elise Jump made a formal confession in the Bibb County jail, which stated she committed the murder unaided.

Indictment and Court Trial

The case was presented at the March 1944 session of the Peach County Grand Jury, which resulted in a true bill. The murder indictment was dated March 7, 1944, and signed by T. A. McCord, grand jury foreman.

The grand jury indictment (number 2218) read in part: "Elise Jump...with an axe, hatchet, and other blunt instruments, and with a knife, dirk, razor, and other sharp instruments...did strike and beat and cut, stab and wound John Jump...thereby giving him a mortal wound."

In addition to foreman T. A. McCord, other grand jurors in the March session were: B. F. O'Neal, T. M. Anthoine, G. G. Adams, A. W. Tabor, J. W. Bradshaw, F. W. Withoft, E. H. Holland, W. D. Thorpe, Jr.,W. H. Wortham, W. T. Pearson, C. H. Matthews, R. C. Evans, S. A. Frederick, R. P. Swan, H. T. Wilder, G. W. Pearson, M. R. Murray, R. D. Gillespie, J. E. Hollingsworth, C. E. McGee, J. D. Kendrick, and W. E. Brisendine.

A week later, the Jump murder case was heard by a criminal jury. Witnesses at the trial were Howard Moore, J. W. Bloodworth,

George Lightfoot, W. H. Beeland, G. W. Cochran, Charlie Adkins, and Mary Bloodworth. On March 16, 1944, the trial jury found Elise Jump guilty. Jury foreman C. L. Shepard Jr. handscribed the verdict, dated March 18, 1944: *"We the jury find the defendant guilty of voluntary manslaughter and fix the penalty at not less than seventeen years or more than twenty years."* Judge George S. Carpenter signed the verdict.

Charles H. Garrett was Solicitor General and Mrs. W. C. McGahee was Prosecutor. Attorney George Garrett defended Mrs. Jump. Superior Court Judge George S. Carpenter, Ocmulgee Circuit, presided over the trial. Superior Court Clerk was J. Leonard Wilson and Lila C. Crawford served as deputy clerk. On March 20, 1944, a motion was filed for a new trial and withdrawn over three months later, on July 7, 1944, by defense counsel George Garrett.

A relative took custody of Mrs. Jump's children during her incarceration. Mrs. Jump reportedly was paroled in 1950. Her whereabouts are unknown. If living, she now would be around ninety years of age.

Were There Accomplices?

The March 23, 1944, issue of the *Leader Tribune* published a provocative quote from Solicitor General Charles Garrett: In asking the jury to return the death verdict, Garrett declared, "I don't believe she did it by herself. The road to the truth leads through her, and we'll never know who is involved unless she tells us."

The observation by Solicitor General Charles Garrett that Elise Jump did not act alone is a distinct possibility. How could Elise Jump, a diminutive ninety-eight-pound woman, have dissected the body of her husband without assistance? First, she would have had to slice through Jump's neck to remove his head. Then she would have had to cut through his thick abdominal cavity while sawing through his backbone.

Could this small woman have dragged the body of her two hundred-pound husband—two parts weighing about a hundred pounds each plus his head—some two hundred yards to the railroad tracks? Who helped her dismember the body, drag the body parts to the railroad tracks in several trips, then come back to the house and clean up all the blood and gore? It is inconceivable she did this alone. Over sixty years have elapsed since the sensational murder, yet people in the Valley are still speculating as to who was

Elise Jump's accomplice. This is a mystery for the ages. Someone evidently helped her, but his identity is a secret that will go to the grave with Elise Jump.

Sources:

Detective Magazine, 1944-provided by Virginia Howard
   (Chief Cochran's daughter)
Police Gazette, circa 1950-provided by Tom Turner of Marshallville
Leader Tribune, 1943-44
Peach County Superior Court Records (case 2218)
   provided by Superior Court Clerk Joe Wilder
Joyce Mason's Research Records
Interviews with local citizens

Chapter 10
The Cold-Bloodied Murder at Blue Bird

The *Leader Tribune,* February 8, 1940, reported the following obituary: "Funeral services for William J. Milburn, 56-year old farmer of Peach County, whose death occurred on Monday (February 5th), were held at 11 a.m. Wednesday (February 7th) at the Mount Zion churchyard cemetery, near Mitchell, Georgia. Milburn had lived in Peach County for about 20 years and operated a farm several miles out on the Perry road. His wife died about a year ago."

The *Leader Tribune* made no mention that Milburn was murdered by Roy Rowland in the parking lot of Blue Bird Body Company in Fort Valley.

Milburn, a middle-aged man, owned a farm on Norwood Springs Road off the Perry Highway, located about four miles south of Fort Valley. He was born and raised in Glascock County and moved to Fort Valley during the early 1920s. According to contemporaries of Milburn, after Milburn's wife died in early 1939, he started attending square dances and round dances held at different locations in Peach County. Reportedly, it was at these

Anderson's Drug Store in 1936. L-R: Malcolm Taylor, Homer Avera, Ben Anderson, Bunch Haslem, and Roy Rowland.

dances where Milburn met Roy Rowland's wife, the former Irene Stembridge, who was in her mid-twenties at the time. Mrs. Rowland was reputed to be an attractive lady by those who remember her. Her husband, Roy, was a clerk at Anderson's Drug Store where he served as stock and delivery man and often worked in the soda fountain. Roy and his wife, Irene, lived on Anderson Avenue, several houses south of the Walden Street intersection. Rowland reportedly built the house himself.

Old timers who lived in Fort Valley at the time state that William Milburn persisted in making overtures to Mrs. Rowland. One man observed that it amounted to stalking. A contemporary lady friend of Mrs. Rowland said that she was a virtuous lady, kind and friendly to everyone. Roy Rowland apparently got fed up with Milburn's pursuit of his wife and plotted to kill him. Roy Rowland knew Milburn's routine. Every morning Milburn would take his son, Charlie, to work at Blue Bird Body Company; then in the afternoon, he would return and pick him up. On the day of the murder, Roy Rowland waited near the traffic light in downtown Fort Valley for Milburn to pass through town.

Urbin Hallman, a friend of Rowland, stated that less than an hour before the murder, that he saw Roy Rowland standing on Main Street in downtown Fort Valley in front of the bank. Hallman recalled, "It was misting rain and Roy was wearing a raincoat. I wondered why he was not at work at the drug store and had stationed himself near the traffic light." After learning of the murder, Hallman reasoned that Rowland had been watching for Milburn to drive through town in his truck, then followed Milburn to Blue Bird.

Urbin Hallman saw Rowland standing in the rain at traffic light.

Another witness was Bill Hopkins, eleven years old at the time, who worked in the soda fountain at Anderson's Drug Store where he came in contact with Roy Rowland. About thirty minutes before the fatal shooting, Hopkins related that Rowland asked Arthur Johnson, who also worked there, if he could borrow his car, a 1939 brown Chevrolet, to run an errand. Apparently, this was immediately after Rowland had seen Milburn pass through town, heading to Blue Bird Body Company to pick up his son from work.

Hopkins recounted that Rowland quickly left the store and drove to Blue Bird. There he parked the 1939 Chevrolet in Blue Bird's parking lot and approached Milburn's vehicle carrying a gun. A verbal exchange ensued and, when Milburn stepped outside his vehicle, Rowland shot Milburn five times in cold blood. Still in a fit of rage, Rowland drew a sharp knife from his pocket. While the dying man was gasping for breath and dying in a puddle of blood, Rowland ripped open Milburn's pants and cut off Milburn's penis. In a gesture of retribution, he laid the penis on Milburn's chest and drove away.

"About thirty minutes later, Roy came back to the store," commented Hopkins. "He walked calmly over to Mr. Homer Avera, a druggist there, and said, 'I just killed a man.'" Sheriff John Lee was called and Rowland was arrested at the store. "Roy was a friend, and a good fella to work with," remarked Hopkins. "I cannot envision Roy committing such a heinous crime."

Slightly after five o'clock on February 5, 1940, Henry Outler, twenty years old at the time, was enroute to Macon with his wife Mary to see the movie *Gone with the Wind*. As he passed by Blue Bird in his car traveling on Highway 49, Henry noticed a large crowd gathering in the plant parking lot where the shooting had taken place. Henry worked at Mr. Homer Duke's Standard Oil service station at Five Points that stood in the triangle across the street from Blue Bird. When Henry returned to work the next morning, the murder at Blue Bird was the talk of the town. Outler remembers seeing William Milburn occasionally, whom he described as just an ordinary man in temperament and stature. "Milburn came from up around Edge Hill, Georgia, near Mitchell, Georgia," stated Outler. "He made his living as a farmer. In those days, you could make a decent living farming on a small scale, but not today." Outler stated that the land Milburn farmed is on the same tract as the Luce Farm today.

Grand Jury Indictment

Charlie Milburn, William J. Milburn's son, signed the official murder charge. After hearing the evidence, the Peach County grand jury issued a true bill, dated March 11, 1940, charging Roy Rowland of Fort Valley with murder.

The grand jury indictment read: "The grand jurors selected, chosen and sworn for the County of Peach...charge and accuse Roy Rowland...with the offense of murder... on the 5th day of February in the year Nineteen Hundred and Forty...with a knife, dirk, razor and other sharp instruments and a pistol, which he had and held, the same being a weapon likely to produce death, make an assault upon W.J. Milburn, and...with said weapon did then and there unlawfully, feloniously, and with malice of aforethought, cut, stab, wound and shoot the said W.J. Milburn, thereby giving him a mortal wound the said, W.J. Milburn, then and there died..."

The twenty-two grand jurors were: J.D. Kendrick-foreman, Al Rock, B.L. Robinson, E.B.Wilson, R.B. Houser, W.D. Thorpe Jr., William J. Wilson, D.W. Wells, W.A. Wood, C.B. Grimes Sr., C.J. Jones, W.G. Brisendine, H.H. Hafer, J.B. Benton, R.A. Hall, Randolph Walker, E.H. Holland, E.L. Duke, W.H. Hopkins, A.B. Young Jr., J.M. Walton, and G.W. Mills. The names of Thorpe, Brisendine, and Hopkins were struck through, indicating they were excused for legal reasons. All members of that grand jury are deceased.

Criminal Trial

The case promptly went to a jury trial. Witnesses were J. Mullis, Bentley Arnold, Leroy Hallman, Carlisle Irby, Charlie Milburn, Mrs. Eddie Lee Adams, Ashby McCord Sr., Miss Lizzie Bowman, and Hubert Yaughn. Following a speedy trial, Roy Rowland was found "not guilty." On March 15, 1940, the trial jury foreman Ed Vinson wrote: "We the jury find the defendant not guilty." Apparently, the trial jury felt Rowland had ample provocation as they ruled him not guilty.

Hallman attended the criminal trial which he said, "went on for four days." Local attorney Billy Lee (Sheriff John Lee's son) defended Rowland, and Solicitor Charles Garrett prosecuted the case. Hallman heard Ashby McCord Sr., owner of funeral home, testify in court on the mutilation of Milburn's body. Hallman stated that, although the crime was obviously premeditated, the jury chose to apply the "unwritten law" in making its ruling. In those days,

Shooting occurred at the Blue Bird parking lot.

Trial was held at the Peach County Courthouse.

juries frowned upon any man who was "messing with" another's wife. A husband who killed another man found in a sexual act with his wife was normally set free. A husband who killed another man who attempted to seduce his wife was also ruled justified.

The night after the trial, Rowland visited Hallman at the

fire station where Hallman worked at night. "Roy told me he was going to get on with his life," said Hallman. Hallman disclosed that Rowland moved to Atlanta and lived on the same street as Hallman's son. Hallman never suspected Rowland would commit such a vicious crime, concluding, "Roy was as nice as he could be. He just ran into a situation that he couldn't control."

Bill Hopkins also confirmed that Rowland moved away and said that Rowland went into the construction business. "Roy Rowland passed from this life around 2000 or 2001, within several months of Dr. Malcolm Taylor's death," observed Hopkins. Incidentally, Dr. Taylor owned a drug store, just up the street from Avera's, on the corner of Main and Macon (now Camellia Street) Streets.

Joe Wilder, current Clerk of the Peach County Superior Court, stated that a transcript of the jury trial is not available. Criminal Record Docket, Book B, page 102 reflects only the case number "1959" and the "Not Guilty" verdict. Since the defendant was ruled not guilty–with no possibility of appeal–the court may have decided not to file an official transcript.

Final thoughts

This story is predicated on evidence gathered from newspaper accounts, court documents, and the testimony of contemporary eyewitnesses. It is readily apparent that Milburn had done something that infuriated Rowland, who was enraged to the point that taking Milburn's life was not enough. He went that extra step in vengeance of depriving the dying man of his manhood by severing his male organ.

As historical research for this book has unfolded, it has become increasing apparent that Fort Valley, during its early days, was not the sleepy, tranquil, uneventful, little hamlet that many had envisioned, but at times was a virtual Peyton Place where murders, criminal acts, and misdeeds were occurring with appalling frequency.

Sources: Peach County Court records
Interviews with local citizens
The *Leader Tribune*

Chapter 11
The Murder of Denise Allison:
Her Killer Walks Among Us

Denise Murray was a popular student during her school days at the Peach County Schools in Fort Valley, had many friends, and was well known in the community. She was the daughter of Ernest and Linda Haywood Murray. Her father, nicknamed "Moose," was a star football player for the Fort Valley High Greenwave from 1948 to 1952, and was considered one of the top offensive and defensive linemen in central Georgia.

During 1982, Denise married a local boy, Bruce Allison, the son of Ed Allison and Patsy Dooley. Their union produced a daughter named Tanya. Bruce was a grandson of James and Lula Dooley, the elder Mr. Dooley being deceased. At the time, Grandmother Dooley had moved in with her daughter in another town. Living in the former Dooley home on Anderson Avenue were Denise, Bruce, and three-year-old Tanya Allison, along with Denise's older sister, Sharon Murray Campbell, and her eighteen-month-old daughter, Leanna.

Both Denise and Bruce Allison worked for Bobby Hester, a Fort Valley City Councilman, who owned three convenience stores in Fort Valley: the number 1 store on Orange Street, number 2 on the Marshallville Highway, and number 3 being the Pump House on the Perry Road. The

Denise and daughter Tanya in 1985.

Pump House was located one mile south of downtown Fort Valley on Highway 341 south, just past the Catholic Church.

Little did the nineteen-year-old Denise Allison know that when she came to work at the Pump House on Wednesday, January 1, 1986, that she would soon be fighting for her life. She was supposed to be off New Year's Day, but a last minute schedule change by the store manager resulted in her working the day shift. As the store's clerk, Denise was responsible for monitoring the gas pumps and ringing up concession sales.

On that fateful New Year's morning, older sister Sharon, age twenty-four, and Denise, nineteen, were getting ready to go to work –Denise at the Pump House at 6:00 a.m. and Sharon at Quality Foods, north of town, at 7:00 a.m. Sharon recalls how impressive Denise looked. "She was wearing a brown silk shirt, blue jeans, tennis shoes, and a brown sweater. "Denise looked so very pretty and I told her so," remarked Sharon.

According to the statement of husband, Bruce Allison, he left about 5:50 a.m. driving Denise to the Pump House, which opened at six o'clock. He said the trip took about five minutes. When they arrived, Bruce asked for a Coke. Denise entered the store and brought it back to the car. Bruce paid Denise seventy-five cents for the drink and Denise reentered the store. Bruce recalled seeing Denise walk behind the counter and hang her purse on the chair. As he drove away, Denise was making her way toward the back of the store to turn on the lights. Bruce observed that no cars were seen around the building or on the street. According to his statement, Bruce drove directly home, arriving about five after six.

Police summoned to Pump House

Corporal Howard Wood of the Fort Valley Police Department, in his incident report, stated that he was dispatched to the Pump House, following a 7:20 a.m. emergency call to the police station made by Pump House customers at a pay phone. He arrived at 7:26 a.m. and was hailed by four males standing by a truck beside the gas pump island. The customers told Corporal Wood that they had stopped to buy gas and had observed a girl lying on the floor inside and that she was obviously hurt very badly. When Wood stepped inside, he saw Denise lying in a pool of blood about her head. Her face was covered with blood and her hair matted with blood. She was still alive, but breathing very shallow. Wood observed a network of puncture marks covering her back. A hammer lay near Denise's head, and a potato hoe lay between her and the bathroom door. Corporal Wood radioed the police dispatcher requesting he call an ambulance, notify the investigator on call, and advise Bobby Hester, the Pump House owner.

Once the EMTs arrived and began working on the victim, Corporal Wood asked them to disturb as little as possible at the crime scene pending arrival of the investigator. Police investigator, Lieutenant Jerry Stripling, arrived shortly afterwards and took charge. Detective Captain Gary Trawick was also called. He went to the hospital to see the victim before joining the other officers at

Pump House in 1986 at time of the murder. Photo courtesy Jarrett Hill.

the Pump House. Corporal Wood found the cash register and the money drawer that was kept under the counter both open. Some change remained, but the paper money had been taken, according to his report. Reported missing was $235. Wood also states that area residents were checked and one possible witness found, a seven-year-old boy, who was taken to the police station for questioning.

Police officer Mary Butler arrived eight minutes later at 7:34 a.m., according to her report. She took the names of the four men who had stopped to purchase gas for their truck. Three men were from Columbus, Georgia: Del Gilley, Robert Lee, and Ronnie Hall, and a fourth, David Snelling, from Phoenix City, Alabama. The four men, working for Wright Way Quality Homes in Warner Robins, were enroute to Marshallville, Georgia, to frame a house. They were staying at the Siesta Motel just outside Fort Valley on U.S. 341 South. Shortly after 7:00 a.m., they left the Siesta motel, a short drive from the Pump House. Ronnie Hall was driving the truck; the other three men were passengers. Hall pulled in at the Pump House to fill up with gasoline and to get a quart of oil. He didn't see anyone inside the Pump House and almost decided to leave; however, since the store's lights were on, he exited the truck to see if the clerk was working in a back room. He went to the door and pulled the handle. The door was open, so he assumed the clerk was inside and went back to pump gas. Then passenger Del Gilley got out of the truck and entered the store to buy a package of cigarettes and to get a cup of coffee. Gilley looked behind the counter and didn't see anyone. He then turned his head toward the other end of the store. There he saw a woman lying on the floor in the aisle by the drink cooler. Gilley immediately rushed out of the store and told his companions that the lady inside was

"messed up pretty bad." Using the pay phone nearby, Ronnie Hall notified the police. The call was received by the police radio dispatcher at 7:20 a.m. Then another passenger in the truck, Dave Snelling, used the pay phone to request an ambulance. Ronnie Hall didn't enter the store, but, after looking in, said he "saw a lady lying on the floor," who "was very bloody." According to Hall, neither he, Robert Lee, nor David Snelling went inside and that only Gilley entered the Pump House.

Crime Scene: notice on the floor the blood stains, potato hoe (far left), tennis shoes, bloody clothes, strewn merchandise, and Michelob box that Allison had opened before being attacked. At rear behind the cooler is the restroom door and at right is the glassed drink cooler.

Corporal Wood, in his report, stated that a struggle had taken place and that many items had been knocked from the shelves, and that blood was smeared on the floor around the south end of the station.

EMTs arrive at the scene

EMTs were dispatched from the Peach County Hospital, just north of town on State Highway 49, and arrived within minutes. By all odds, Denise shouldn't have been alive when the EMTs arrived. Realizing that quick action was necessary, Donnie Martin and Alfonso Ford administered emergency aid to Denise on the spot, and then transported her to the Peach County Hospital. There Dr. George Shoup performed surgery to stop internal bleeding and to repair a punctured lung…and to buy Denise more time. Following surgery, Denise was carried by ambulance to the Medical Center of Central Georgia in Macon and admitted at 2:26 p.m. on that same day, where a neurosurgeon, Dr. Sam Robinson Jr., performed surgery to remove skull fragments from her brain resulting from the heavy hammer blows to the head inflicted by the assailant.

Police investigation and manhunt begins

Other police officers arrived on the scene within minutes after notification. In a short time, officers with bloodhounds from the Houston County K-9 Unit began searching the area, combing a radius of two-and-a-half miles from the Pump House. Although several promising leads were developed, the search was called off at 9:30 that night, January 1, 1986, and resumed the next day.

The local investigation was led by Detective Captain Gary Trawick and Lieutenant Jerry Stripling of the Fort Valley Police Department, both certified as crime scene investigators. At the time, the police department was without its police chief, John Dankel, who had resigned the previous month, December 1985, to become an instructor at the Georgia Police Academy in Atlanta, Georgia. Major Otis Green was made acting police chief.

Detective Captain Trawick stated that over one hundred pieces of evidence, including fingerprints, blood samples, and hair fibers, were collected at the crime scene over a 24-hour period by himself and Detective Lieutenant Jerry Stripling. Also

Knife handle, hammer and hoe used in assault. Victim was hit so hard with hoe, the prongs were bent.

bagged as evidence were the knife handle and blade found in restroom, and the garden hoe and claw hammer found lying by Denise's body. All the evidence gathered was sent to the crime lab in Atlanta for processing.

GBI incident report

According to the incident report filed by the Region 13 office of the Georgia Bureau of Investigation (reporting officer, Robert S. Smith, and approving officer, Jack H. White) on January 14, 1986, "the victim was found about 7:30 a.m." and had been "beaten with a claw hammer and a hoe"...and... "was found lying in a pool of blood"..."by customers who came to the store to buy gas." The report states the cash register was emptied with $173 taken, except for a "$1 bill that would have triggered the surveillance camera."

This conflicts with the police report, which stated that "no paper money" was in either the cash register or the money

drawer kept under the counter. Further, the police report states that $235 was taken. According to the former Chief Deputy Sheriff Jimmy Jones, who participated in the investigation, the surveillance camera—which used Polaroid film--had not been loaded with film; consequently, no pictures would have been available of the suspect had the camera been activated.

The robber, evidently with prior knowledge of how the camera worked, left a one dollar bill in cash register to prevent the surveillance camera from being activated.

Denise was lying in the aisle near the beer and drink cooler and in proximity to the restroom at the south end of the store. Indicative that part of the assault occurred in the restroom was a bloody hand print found just above the light switch. Also, the lid had been knocked off the commode. After knocking Denise unconscious, the assailant emptied the cash register and money drawer and fled the scene, obviously wearing bloody

Detective Captain Gary Trawick led the investigation.

clothes and shoes. Blood was all over the floor and on the merchandise. Police chief investigator, Captain Gary Trawick, stated that the keys to the store were found under the candy counter.

"This was not a normal murder... someone had it in for her."–Officer Robinson

The *Leader Tribune* reported that Denise was seen inside the Pump House by Fort Valley Police Department officer Arnold Robinson not long after she opened the store at 6:00 a.m. Officer Robinson was making his early morning rounds in the police cruiser. When he drove past the Pump House he saw the lights on, but didn't see the clerk inside. Feeling disquieted, Robinson turned around at Lavender Street and drove back to the Pump House. He still didn't see the clerk inside. As he began to exit his car to check the store, Denise stood up near the drink cooler and waved to indicate she was okay. Robinson waved back and drove away, continuing to check other businesses along the highway. This interchange between Robinson and Allison occurred about 6:30 a.m.

Shortly after Officer Robinson made his drive-through security check—possibly within minutes—someone entered the store, stabbed Denise with a knife that broke, then brutally beat her with a potato hoe (having two metal prongs on the end opposite the blade) and finally delivered lethal blows to her head with a claw hammer.

After the knife broke, possibly inside the restroom (where it was found), the assailant went into a frenzy as the struggle ensued outside the restroom and stabbed her over fifty times in her upper torso with the pronged end of the hoe, drawing blood with each thrust and puncturing her lungs. The assailant flailed away so hard with the hoe that he chipped away chunks of the ceiling tile with his backswings. From all indications, Denise tried valiantly to fend off the blows and put up one hell of a fight trying to defend herself. Finally, the assailant beat her on the head with the claw hammer. He kept swinging until he crushed in the right side of her skull. Blood was all over the store from the cash register at the front to the bathroom on the far side of the store.

Officer Robinson now works for the Taylor County Sheriff's Department. "The murder occurred during an extremely tight time frame," observed Robinson. Robinson, whose shift started at 6:00 a.m., recalls that he saw Denise stocking the drink cooler inside the Pump House around 6:30 a.m. The Pump House was about one-and-a-quarter miles from the police station. Robinson knew Denise's father, Moose Murray, who he said was "a fine fella," but did not have an acquaintance with Denise. Not long after Robinson returned to the police station, he heard that a robbery and assault had occurred at the Pump House.

Robinson doesn't believe that robbery was a motive. "This was not a normal killing," said Robinson. "She was killed deliberately. Someone had it in for her."

Timeline for Murder

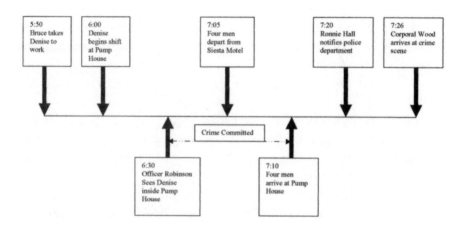

| 5:50 Bruce takes Denise to work | 6:00 Denise begins shift at Pump House | | 7:05 Four men depart from Siesta Motel | | 7:20 Ronnie Hall notifies police department | 7:26 Corporal Wood arrives at crime scene |

Crime Committed

| | 6:30 Officer Robinson Sees Denise inside Pump House | 7:10 Four men arrive at Pump House | |

Denise Allison dies after being comatose for six days

Early Thursday, January 2, Denise's condition improved somewhat as she briefly regained consciousness and squeezed the hands of family members to affirm that she recognized and loved them. She was unable, however, to talk and identify her assailant. Saturday night, January 4, she took a turn for the worse. She became comatose and was placed on life support. On the following Monday, January 6, after tenaciously clinging to life for six days, Denise was declared clinically brain dead. A decision was deferred until Tuesday morning about withdrawing life support. Before Tuesday dawned, God in His mercy called Denise home.

Denise Allison's Funeral

Funeral services for Denise Allison were held at Chamlee Memorial Baptist Church in Fort Valley, Georgia, on January 9, 1986. Rev. Mervin Watford officiated.

Rev. Mervin Watford, who married Denise Murray and Bruce Allison, wrote in his column in the *Leader Tribune* on January 15, 1986, that Mrs. Linda Murray had experienced nightmares about Denise

Denise Murray Allison was a sweet and pretty girl with a promising future, and a three year old daughter to raise.

for many years. "She would dream of Denise being in a terrible accident or drowning," wrote Rev. Watford. "She would reach out her hands for her daughter only to awaken without her." Rev. Watford concluded, "God had prepared Denise's parents that their daughter's life would not be a long one."

Reward established

The *Leader Tribune* on January 8, 1986, devoted its entire front page to the story. The community was shocked with the brutality of the crime. Denise Murray Allison was a precious young lady, loved and respected by all. Local citizens wanted the perpetrator of the crime apprehended and justice served. In response, local merchants and private citizens quickly donated twenty-eight hundred dollars. Governor Joe Frank Harris added two thousand, bringing the total to forty-eight hundred. It would be paid to anyone providing information leading to the apprehension of the assailant.

Bruce Allison's Statement

Bruce disclosed that he and Denise didn't go to a New Year's party the night before and that Denise went to bed early. "She went to bed with the chickens and got up with the chickens," stated Bruce in his recorded interview with the police. He also volunteered that there was no argument the night before. Sharon Murray, Denise' sister, stated that Denise seemed happy that morning as she was preparing to leave for work.

Bruce, an employee of Bobby Hester at his other convenience stores, disclosed that Denise's store opening routine would involve first checking the cooler to see what beer brands needed restocking, and to keep the door locked until a customer came up. If still dark, she would let the customer in and relock the door after the customer exited. According to Bruce, Sharon Murray was up and kept their daughter, Tanya, while he took Denise to work. When asked if Denise or he had used any type of drugs, Bruce stated that neither he nor Denise had ever dealt with dope and that Denise didn't even smoke, much less use any type of drugs.

Sharon Murray Campbell's Statement

Sharon Murray in her statement volunteered that there was no party or other type celebration going on in the house on

New Year's Eve. Sharon went to bed between 10:00 and 10:30 p.m. on December 31, 1985, and arose between 5:00 and 5:30 a.m. on New Year's Day. Sharon heard Bruce and Denise leave the house around 6:00 a.m. Sharon left home about 6:40 a.m. and arrived about 6:45 a.m. at her place of employment, Quality Foods, on Highway 341, north of town. No one was at the store to let her in. She stayed outside Quality Foods until seven o'clock and then returned home. Bruce Allison was in the bed asleep when she returned home. According to Sharon's statement, she was not sure whether Bruce had returned before she left at 6:40 a.m. or whether his car was parked outside when she left. Sharon started calling Quality Foods to see when it would open. About 7:35 a.m., Melba Hester, Bobby Hester's wife, called and asked to speak with Bruce. Sharon summoned Bruce to the phone. Mrs. Hester told Bruce that Denise had been hurt in a robbery and assault at the Pump House. Bruce immediately jumped in the car and drove to the Pump House. Sharon Murray described family life between Bruce and Denise as very good and did not believe that Denise or Bruce had been running around or having an extramarital affair.

Three other renters lived at Allison home on Anderson Avenue

According to GBI reports, there were three other residents at the home of Bruce and Denise Allison on Anderson Avenue who were renters: Billy Stuckey, Terry Albritton, and Albritton's wife, Brenda Michelle Sheffield Albritton. None of the three knew of any arguments or fights between Bruce and Denise Allison. All three were sound asleep when Bruce left carrying Denise to work and when Bruce returned. All three testify to being awakened when the phone rang about 7:35 a.m. notifying Bruce of the robbery and assault at the Pump House.

Terry Albritton, in his statement to the GBI on January 23, 1986, disclosed that Bruce Allison told him he was going to leave Fort Valley for two to three weeks. After being gone only two or three days, according to Albritton, Bruce came back and said everyone had to move, that he (Bruce Allison) had obtained a job in Americus. Allison was visited by GBI Agent S. R. Smith and Chief Deputy Sheriff Jimmy Jones on February 20, 1986, at his residence in Albany, Georgia, where he lived with his brother, Luke Allison. Bruce Allison was asked why he left Fort Valley so soon after Denise's death. Bruce replied that "every time he would go to the Pump House, he would have visions of her lying on the floor."

He also stated he needed someone to help raise their child, Tanya, and that he had more family in Albany than in Fort Valley. Bruce also told the officers that he left "because of the numerous rumors that were flying around Fort Valley."

Bobby Hester's statement

According to Bobby Hester, former owner of the Pump House, even though a clerk opened the store at 6:00 a.m., they would not open the door for regular business until seven, and would use that hour to restock the beer and drink cooler, which evidently Denise was doing at the time. Hester remembers seeing an opened case of Michelob beer on the floor near the cooler when he arrived at the crime scene. He also recalls that a pint carton of chocolate

Denise Allison left her brown purse hanging on the stool at the front counter when she opened the store. The brown coat she wore to work and had placed on the stool was missing when the police arrived at the crime scene.

milk was sitting on the counter at cash register when he arrived soon after police. "That seemed strange," remarked Hester. "I don't believe Denise drank chocolate milk."

Confirming Hester's policy concerning store opening time, Sharon Murray Campbell, Denise's older sister, reiterated that Denise would not open the door before 7:00 a.m. unless someone she knew asked to get in. From all indications, someone Denise knew entered the store and killed her.

The hoe used as a weapon by the assailant was kept in the storage room at the back of the store, according to owner Hester. This is a fact the average customer would not have known. Only someone familiar with the store would have known the location of the hoe.

The hammer used to deliver the fatal blows was kept under the counter near the cash register. Since Denise had been robbed twice at the Pump House the previous year, she kept the hammer close by as a defensive weapon. During the police investigation of an earlier theft, Denise had commented to Detective Captain Trawick: "I will give a robber anything he wants, but I will not let someone rape me." The possibility exists that someone tried to force Denise into the restroom and rape her, accounting for the lid being knocked off the commode and the bloody handprint on the restroom wall. Based upon the struggle moving from the front to the back of the store and its duration, it is obvious that Denise fiercely defended herself and seriously tested the will of the assailant. The extended struggle plus the fact that her killer had to resort to three weapons, a knife, a hoe, and a hammer to subdue her, indicates that he may not have been a big, powerful man. Denise was five feet, seven inches, weighed about 125 pounds, and was capable of putting up a good fight.

New Year's Eve Party held near Pump House

On January 10, 1986, GBI Special Agent R. A. Smith and Sheriff Department Investigator Terry Deese interviewed Theresa Richardson, a nearby resident. Richardson stated that a New Year's Eve party was held at her house. Her house was located on the south side of the Pump House—a chain link fence ran between the end of her backyard and the Pump House. The attendees involved herself, Bruce Day, Betty McAfee, Gregory Lewis, George Waters, and several children. The party lasted until 5:30 a.m. the next morning. Theresa Richardson said that she arose when her seven-year-old son, Tecovian, got up some time after 6:00 a.m. Richardson saw her little son go to the bathroom after he got up, then he went to the back part of the house, and began playing with a remote controlled car. Later, while playing, little Tecovian Richardson looked out the window and saw a man in their backyard. When questioned at the police station by Lieutenant Stripling and Corporal Wood, Tercovian reported that he saw a male figure come running around the south side of Pump House and pass through his backyard. His sighting of the suspect is estimated to have occurred slightly before 7:00 a.m.

Richardson stated that Gregory Lewis and George Waters left the house about 7:30 a.m. She stated that either Lewis or Waters told her they had seen a truck outside the Pump House when they departed—evidently the truck carrying the men who found the victim. Bruce Day, also a resident of the house, stated he did not get up early and had no knowledge of the crime other than what people told him. Betty McAfee, also a resident there, stated that she had not seen or heard anything out of the ordinary at the Pump House on New Year's morning.

Georgia Bureau of Investigation requested to assist in investigation

The day after the murder, January 2, 1986, Detective Trawick called in Jay Jarvis, a crime scene investigator from the Macon crime lab. On January 7, 1986, the Assistant District Attorney in Fort Valley, Wayne "Biff" Tillis, requested the Region 13 GBI office in Perry, Georgia, to assist with the investigation.

Arrest of Suspect

A composite sketch of the suspect, from witness descriptions, was produced by late Thursday afternoon, January 2, 1986. The suspect's sketch on the front page of the *Leader Tribune*, on January 8, depicted a black man with a mustache, short beard, and steely, menacing eyes. He was described as being 5'8" to 6' 0" tall and weighing approximately 180 pounds. This sketch, according to the local newspaper, reportedly resembled a man who was seen in the area driving a red van bearing an expired Dade County temporary vehicle tag. Detective Trawick was quoted in the *Leader Tribune* as saying the sketch closely matched the features of Willie G. Nelms, age thirty-three, of Miami, Florida, who reportedly drove a red blazer and, at the time, was staying in Fort Valley at the Siesta Motel on U.S. Highway 341 south of Fort Valley.

On January 13, 1986, after issuance of a warrant by Probate Judge John W. "Buddy" Smisson, Detective Trawick and Terry Deese traveled to Miami, Florida, to gather physical evidence from Willie G. Nelms, age thirty-three. Nelms, who worked for the City of Miami as a heavy equipment maintenance worker, submitted voluntarily to questioning and allowed investigators to take his fingerprints and collect blood and hair samples. He also was administered polygraph tests.

According to the handwritten statement of Willie Nelms in the case file, witnessed and signed by Detective Gary Trawick, Nelms arrived in Fort Valley on New Year's Eve, December 31, 1985, at approximately 8:00 p.m. He went to his girlfriend's mother's house on East Main Street and stayed there until 10:00 to 10:30

p.m. That same night, he and his girlfriend attended church on Preston Street. They left church around 12:30 to 1:00 a.m. on New Year's Day, January 1, rode around for a while, and then he took his girlfriend home to East Main Street.

During the wee morning hours of January 1, Nelms drove to Perry, Georgia, twelve miles away, and entered a convenience store to purchase hotdogs and Gator Aid. Nelms tried to buy beer, but the "guy wouldn't sell it." According to Nelms' statement, he returned to the Siesta Motel in Fort Valley and went to sleep. When he arose the next morning (still January 1), he went to the Siesta Motel office and paid for another day. Nelms went back to his motel room and watched television until around noon January 1, then went back to his girlfriend's house. He and his girlfriend spent the night of January 1 at the motel.

The next day, January 2, Nelms and his girlfriend visited friends at Fort Valley State College and afterwards loaded up his red blazer, leaving town at approximately eleven a.m. and heading back to Miami, Florida.

Willie Nelms Arrested on murder warrant

Two months later, on March 19, 1986, Probate Court Judge "Buddy" Smisson issued a murder warrant against Willie G. Nelms, age thirty-three, of Miami, Florida. The magistrate case number was 5150 CR12 P2, and the applicable code section of Georgia law was 16-5-1. Witnesses listed on the warrant were Captain Gary Trawick, Peach County Sheriff Johnnie Becham, and Sergeant Jim West of the Perry Police Department.

On Saturday, March 22, 1986, Nelms was arrested in Miami by Captain Trawick and Lieutenant Jerry Stripling, brought back to Fort Valley, and placed in the Peach County jail. No commitment hearing was held for Nelms. According to Detective Trawick, he urged the District Attorney to hold the commitment hearing and to have another suspect, Ronnie Smith, testify of his knowledge of the murder. According to the official transcript of the preliminary hearing before the Magistrate Court on March 28, 1986, Ronnie Smith had identified Willie Nelms as the assailant from a photo line-up (reference pages 11, 22, 25, 30, 31, and 40 of transcript).

Nelms Released

Willie Nelms was represented by Fort Valley attorney Gregory Homer. After the state crime lab rendered its report,

Assistant District Attorney Wayne "Biff" Tillis stated that the lab tests failed to link Nelms to the crime. After reviewing the evidence, District Attorney Willis Sparks stated that he would advise Superior Court Judge C. Cloud Morgan that the state did not have sufficient credible evidence to proceed with a commitment hearing for Nelms. Consequently, on April 2, 1986, in a meeting with Judge C. Cloud Morgan requested by the District Attorney's office, the murder warrant against Nelms was dismissed. The dismissal bears Judge Morgan's signature.

The fact that it was dismissed without a hearing surprised the Fort Valley Police Department. Frank Strickland, who became police chief during mid-March 1986, said his office was never notified by the District Attorney's office that Nelms would be released. Captain Trawick stated that, before a murder warrant was dismissed, it was customary for the District Attorney to hold a hearing before the superior court judge with the affected law enforcement authorities in attendance. In this instance the District Attorney's office took the action unilaterally. Following his release, Nelms returned to his home in Miami.

Nelms's attorney files suit in federal district court

Almost two years later, on January 17, 1988, a case (nr. 5:88-CV-69) was filed in the Federal District Court in Macon, Georgia, with Willie Gene Nelms as plaintiff, charging the City of Fort Valley with a civil rights violation. Cited in the suit were police officers Trawick and Stripling, its city council members and mayor, Pete Peterson. The $2 million suit claimed that the plaintiff was falsely arrested without probable cause. Nelms's attorney contended that the evidence presented to the court was manufactured. Representing Nelms was attorney Gregory Homer of Fort Valley. Listed as representing the city were attorneys Charles Adams of Fort Valley and Charles (Chuck) Byrd of Perry. On February 28, 1991, Judge Duross Fitzpatrick issued an order referring the case to mediation. James B. Chaplin of Fort Lauderdale, Florida, was named as mediator. An out-of-court settlement was mutually agreed upon and fixed at $135,000. On April 8, 1991, a voluntary dismissal was issued by Judge Fitzpatrick.

Ronnie Smith tells Perry Police officers
he has knowledge of Pump House killing

During March 1986, Ronnie Jerome Smith, age twenty-five, a resident of 126 Peachtree Street in Fort Valley, was arrested for attempted car burglary (stealing equipment from cars) in Perry, Georgia, and incarcerated in the Perry city jail. Smith had been charged with a previous burglary in Warner Robins during December 1985.

On March 15, 1986, Smith indicated to the arresting officer, Sgt. Jim West of Perry, that he had information on the assault at the Pump House in Fort Valley. Officer West notified Detective Gary Trawick, who drove to Perry on March 17, 1986, to interview Smith.

Suspect's testimony places him
inside the Pump House during assault of Allison

Included in the Fort Valley Police Department case file no. 13-0248-01-86, obtained through an open records request, are eight statements provided by Ronnie Smith concerning his knowledge of the Pump House murder: four handwritten and four tape-recorded. Based on his statements, Smith witnessed the assault against Denise Allison, (whom he had known from his school days) inside the Pump House. He saw the killer face-to-face. Smith is quoted by police officers as saying that the assailant was a black male whom he had seen several times on the streets of Fort Valley, at the Spruce Street gym, and that he possibly was a boyfriend of a girl whose last name was Thomas.

On the morning of the murder, Smith said that he knocked on the locked door of the Pump House before it opened for business and that Denise opened the door. Corroborating this is an excerpt from a typed statement, dated March 18, 1986, at 11:25 p.m., by Sgt. Jim West of the Perry Police Department, which places Smith inside the Pump House while the assault is taking place:

Smith accompanied by Officer Bray, Officer Hathcock, and myself (Sgt. West) went to the Pump House in Fort Valley and were met by Captain Trawick, Chief Strickland, and Sheriff Becham. After being advised of his rights to have an attorney present, Smith ultimately walked us through the events and stated that he had gone to the Pump House and was admitted by Denise Allison. He asked for a quart of beer which she consented to let him have, and then asked if he could use the restroom. As he was walking toward the restroom, he saw a black male who he had identified walking toward the front door in the opposite direction. He (Smith) entered the restroom and heard a voice say, "Give me the money." When he (Smith) came out of the restroom, the black male was striking

Denise and they were scuffling. He (Smith) went back into the restroom and got a hoe and came back and tried to defend her when the black man hit him in the left side. The struggle swept him into the restroom ahead of the clerk and the black man. He ran out the door (of Pump House) and then got back inside where the black man came after him."

Detective Captain Trawick's statement

Detective Captain Gary Trawick of the Fort Valley Police Department, in his statement, recaps the same basic information as Sgt. Jim West with exception of the following excerpts: *"Ronnie (Smith) stated that Denise (Allison) was hit with the side of the hammer and not the front part. He (Smith) pointed to the area behind (Perry Police) Officer Hathcock's right ear as the location of the last blow with the hammer. Ronnie stated that he then took the jacket and put it on to cover the blood on his shirt, and he went to his girlfriend's grandmother's house and washed the blood off his hands and then to his mother's house and burned the bloody clothes in the trash can in the backyard. He gave his shoes and jacket to his girlfriend. Before leaving the store (following a walk-through of the crime on March 18, 1986), Ronnie stated that the handprint in blood on the bathroom wall was his handprint and that it was blood from Denise's head."*

Final statement by Smith

After making both written and tape recorded statements that were constantly changing in details provided, the final statement made by Ronnie Smith, which was tape-recorded and transcribed "verbatim," is reflected below. Smith's statement begins as he enters the Pump House and recounts very graphically the assault of Denise Allison:

"I walked up to the store and I knocked at the glass door. Denise noticed me and she opened the door...I asked her for a free quart of beer. She agreed. She said she would give it to me. After that I said, 'Denise can I use the restroom?' She said, 'yeah.' She said she'd have the beer bagged by the time I had gotten out. She walked back to finish stocking the cooler. I was walking back and I seen this guy coming towards the store.

"After going into the bathroom, I heard the door open, and somebody come in. I heard him say, 'Where's the money?' I heard Denise reply she doesn't have any money...I heard him hit her a

couple of times. After I finished using the restroom, I opened the door and I seen him hit her with his left hand. He had a hammer in his right hand. They started tussling for a second, then I heard Denise reply, 'Ronnie, help me.' The guy had his back toward the bathroom door, and I looked in the bathroom, and grabbed a hoe. The hoe was lying handle down. After I grabbed it, I hit him with an overhand, overhand swing. It must not have had much effect, because after that he turned around and hit me in the ribs, side. It was enough to knock the wind out of me and enough for me to drop the hoe, and I grabbed my side. He was about to hit me again, and I grabbed his arm. Then I just walked back a little bit after I let him go. After that he turned around; he hit Denise with the hammer a couple of times. Denise grabbed him and they started tussling. Still holding my side, then at that time Denise was back to support me, and I was trying to push Denise out of the way, but he had a kind of hold with his left arm, cause he grabbed her. After that I hit him with my fist, missing Denise. I had to reach over her and do it. After that we began backing up to the bathroom. Denise began bleeding from the head.

"At that point, we had, they had backed up to the bathroom, and I was still trying to push Denise out of the way, and we were still struggling and stuff, hammer still in his hand. After going to the bathroom, he hit her once more. I then put my right hand on Denise's hand and hit him with my left hand. Then I grabbed, wrapped my left arm around, and we pushed him out of the way, enough to get out of the (bathroom) door. I grabbed the (bathroom) door with my left hand, put my right hand on the wall, and I ran outside (store). He then turned Denise a loose and began to run after me. He didn't come out of the store. He didn't get very far before Denise had started (to) come out of the bathroom again, and I was about like (near) the sign outside (the store), and I seen him hit her again with the hammer. At that time they had made it (from the bathroom) to the cooler.

"After dropping the hammer, he picked up the hoe. Knowing that he was hitting her, I had seen the hoe go up in the air a few times, like short strokes, like he was bending over. After that I seen him, drop the hoe, and then go back and get the hammer, and I seen him kneel down. At that point, I didn't know what he was doing, so I decided I wanted to go back and help. I got up to the window; I didn't go in first, I just leaned over, peeped in the glass window, and I seen him hit her in the face, in the cranial above the right side of the face. He hit her hard, and then I left the window and started to go into the (front) door. I took about two steps with my left hand still holding the *(front) door inside and I looked. At that time, he hit her the last time with the hammer sideways on top of the skull. He hit her so hard, blood just squirted and started running, and I was like in a state of shock for a minute; I didn't know what to do. Then I said to him; I said 'Damn man, why did you do something like that?'*

"After that he rested for a minute, then he got up and ran after me. He didn't come out of the store. Still I ran back to the sign about in front on the Bowyer's (house) about to the gasoline sign. I seen him look back and seen him reach over the counter; then he began to come out the store, and I ran. He came out of the store and ran behind the Pump House...I had spots of blood on my shirt. I still wanted to call somebody, but I know if I went to somebody's house, they would kind of knot up or something. Call the police; they would expected I did it. So I just left, stopped again, and wanted to go back. So I just ran around Davison Street, back to (my girlfriend's) grandmother's house. At that time, I had a little bit of blood on my hands, very little. I then went to the faucet on the side of the house and washed it off. I went back outside the road and stood up. I had gotten my jacket from off the porch, and I put it on to keep anybody from seeing red, (or looking) suspicious, while I was going down the road.

"After that I was standing on the road, I seen this guy coming through this path, which was behind the house to the right of the Pump House. He had blood stains on his light blue shirt, like in front of the shirt around the stomach area; it was kinda like heavily stained, and then I seen him get out of the path. He had on Converse white All-Star tennis shoes. After getting out of the path (behind Pump House), he ran behind this red house, then he stopped and kneeled down, and I ran up and asked him, 'What was wrong wid you?' He then looked up, called me a son-of-a-bitch and attempted to run after me again. He only attempted, but he didn't. So I ran back down the road, looked back to see where he was, and he had disappeared again...

"We (Smith and girlfriend) went back over to my parent's house. I get into the house about something to eight (A.M.) when we got there. I had taken my shirt off and changed, took it outside and burned it. After that I came back inside and (my sister) asked me had I heard what happened. It was a minute before I said anything, then she explained to me what happened at the Pump House. I told her I was glad she wasn't working, then my mom, she asked me if I had anything to do with this. I replied, 'No.' Quite a few times that I wonder why, why didn't I just turn around and help, why didn't I call somebody."

Later in his taped statement, Ronnie Smith states: *"I am willing to go before the people of Fort Valley and Denise's parents, my parents, the judge and the jury and to tell the truth, the whole truth, so help me God."*

In his concluding remarks, Smith attested to the truth of his final statement that was taped, transcribed, and documented: *"After making this statement, which is true. This statement will never be changed again. This statement is complete. This statement has come to an end. The only thing that hadn't come to an end is the moment when I get to testify, the moment I brings him down. That will be the end of everything."*

Ronnie Smith charged with murder

On March 19, 1986, a murder warrant (Magistrate Case No. 5149 CR12 P1) was issued against Ronnie J. Smith by Probate Court Judge John W. "Buddy" Smisson. Witnesses were Captain Gary Trawick, Peach County Sheriff Johnny Becham, and Sergeant Jim West of the Perry Police Department.

Hearing: State of Georgia vs. Ronnie Smith on murder charge, CCR No. A-104G

Testifying in the hearing at the Magistrate Court on March 28, 1986, were Detective Gary Trawick of the Fort Valley Police Department and Sergeant Jim West of the Perry Police Department. Representing the state was Assistant District Attorney, Wayne G. "Biff" Tillis. Local Fort Valley attorney Alvin McDougald represented Ronnie Smith. The chief magistrate, Judge George Harris, presided. In both the questioning phase and cross-examinations, the two law enforcement officers, Trawick and West, testified of the statements Ronnie Smith made regarding the assault at the Pump House. Summarized below are excerpts from their testimony:

Smith first said he was coming across the parking lot of the Pump House when he saw a male inside the store swinging a hoe. He walked up to the door, looked in the window and saw Denise Allison on the floor. He then saw the black male hit Denise twice on the head with the hammer. Smith became afraid and fled to his girlfriend's house on Davidson Street, approximately two hundred feet behind the Pump House. (pages 5 and 6 of hearing transcript).

His second statement, issued the next day, placed him inside the Pump House where he stood and watched the assault. Then he became fearful and ran. When Smith got back around to Davison Street, he saw the black assailant come down a path behind the Pump House. The man, with blood on his blue pullover shirt, stopped and kneeled momentarily. Smith walked up to the man and asked what was wrong. The man looked at Smith and called him a "son-of-a-bitch," then started chasing Smith. Smith ran to his girlfriend's grandmother's house on Davison Street. (pages 7, 8, and 30 of transcript.)

Smith's third statement was more detailed. On March 18, 1986, around 11:00 p.m, after being advised of his rights, Smith carried law enforcement officers (West, Bray, and Hathcock, from Perry and Captain Trawick, Chief Strickland, and Sheriff Becham) on a walk-through of the Pump House, providing a graphic account of the assault, which was audio-taped. Smith testified that he came to the Pump House on New Year's morning, knowing that Denise would give him a free beer. Smith stated that Denise, his sister, and a cousin that worked there always gave him free beer. Smith knocked on the door. Denise was stocking the beer coolers. Denise came over, unlocked the door, and let Smith in. Smith asked for a quart of beer, to which she agreed. Smith asked to use the restroom. While inside the restroom, he heard an argument and someone said, "Give me your money." When Smith opened the door, he saw a black male striking Denise Allison with his fist. Smith got the hoe that was stored in the bathroom and came out into the store. According to both Detective Trawick and Sergeant West of the Perry Police Department, Smith stated that he hit Denise twice with the hoe. Smith's attorney pointed out that Smith's testimony of hitting Allison was not on tape and not written down in his statement, yet both Trawick and West reiterated that they were positive that Smith said it. (pages 10, 21, 33, 34, 44, and 45 of transcript). Then Smith dropped the hoe, and he and the other male got into a fight. Smith swerved and threw the other black male and Denise into the restroom, and then ran out the front door. Smith stated that the bloody handprint on the bathroom wall was his; that the blood came from Denise's head. (page 10) When Smith left the store, he picked up Allison's jacket from behind the counter, and put it on to conceal the blood on his shirt. (The brown hooded-jacket that Denise Allison wore to work was missing at the crime scene.) Smith then went to his girlfriend's grandmother's house, washed the blood from his hands. He took off his clothes, put them in a trash can in the backyard and burned them. He then gave his girlfriend the jacket and his shoes. (pages 10 , 11, and 23 of transcript)

Smith described the exact position in which Denise Allison's body had been lying, something that only an eyewitness to the crime would have known. (page 11 of transcript)

Smith described the other black man as being around six feet tall, 180 to 210 pounds, heavy, fat faced, short hair, and unshaved. He was stocky-built and wearing a bluish green shirt. (pages 18, 39, and 42 of transcript).

Credibility of Smith's testimony questioned by his attorney

Smith would add more details and progressively involve himself at the crime scene every time he gave his testimony. His lawyer, Alvin McDougald, argued at the hearing in Magistrate Court that "the case basically boils down to the believability of Mr. Smith." (page 51 of hearing transcript) Attorney McDougald further implied that Smith would change his testimony in response to questions by Captain Trawick and Sheriff Becham, but officer Trawick responded, "Ronnie would hesitate, saying the reason he couldn't get it out was that his conscience was bothering him and his conscience was blocking him from telling the truth." (pages 19 and 20 of transcript) McDougald asked Trawick, "Did Mr. Smith at some point in time tell you that everything he told you was made up?" Trawick responded, "At one point he did, and said that he had a lapse... that his conscience was bothering him and he had to get it straight." (page 22 of transcript)

Smith bound over to the Grand Jury

After conducting the above hearing, Chief Magistrate Judge George W. Harris, on March 28, 1986, bound Smith over to the next term of the Grand Jury without any bond. The charge was murder in accordance with Georgia Code 16-5-1.

Corroborating statements by GBI agents

An official statement by GBI Special Agent Allen Smith, dated March 21, 1986, states that Smith "met a black male subject with blood on his clothes running down the path behind the Pump House on January 1, 1986," and that "Smith identified Willie Nelms from a photo lineup." This information was provided Special Agent Smith by Jimmy Jones of the Peach County Sheriff's Office who had conferred with Sgt. Jim West of the Perry Police

Department, where Smith was under arrest for attempted theft from an automobile.

GBI Special Agent R.A. Smith filed the following report on March 20, 1986, at 8:45 a.m.: "Assistant District Attorney W.G. 'Biff' Tillis advised that the subject, Ronnie Smith, who was being held in the Perry Police Department jail, had on further questioning changed his story from the initial report that he had seen a black male running from the Pump House on January 1, 1986. Smith had stated in supplemental interviews that he had been present when the attack had taken place. However, Smith did not state that he was in any way involved in the robbery and the assault of Denise Allison. Smith had stated that he was a witness to the crime and had identified Willie Nelms as the person who had committed the crime. Tillis stated that warrants had been taken for (Ronnie) Smith and for Willie Nelms in Miami, Florida. Tillis stated that several tape-recordings had been made of statements given by Ronnie Smith and these tape-recorded statements were being reviewed."

On March 20, 1986, at 11:30 a.m., GBI Special Agent R. A. Smith contacted Assistant District Attorney W. G. "Biff" Tillis at his office in Fort Valley. Excerpts from his report follows: "Tillis provided copies of statements of Ronnie Smith which had been turned over to him...It is noted that all of the statements were in the handwriting of Ronnie Smith. According to Tillis, these (handwritten) statements were really not useful in any prosecution against Ronnie Smith. According to Tillis, Alvin McDougald (Fort Valley Attorney) has consulted with Ronnie Smith in the Perry Police Department jail. It is not known at this time whether McDougald will represent Ronnie Smith. Tillis stated that he had reviewed the taped statements. He stated in these (taped) statements, there was still not sufficient evidence to prosecute Ronnie Smith. Tillis stated that Detective Trawick was enroute to Florida to pick up Willie Nelms and that all the taped statements had been taken by Trawick to Florida. "

Suspect Ronnie Smith released

In early June 1986, Attorney Alvin McDougald of Fort Valley, who represented Ronnie Smith, petitioned Judge C. Cloud Morgan to release his client on a $10,000 bond. Judge Morgan concurred, ruling that there was insufficient evidence for the prosecution to continue opposition to the bond. Smith was allowed to post

Assistant District Attorney Wayne "Biff" Tillis stated that the suspects were released because there was "no forensic, physical, or corroborative evidence to implicate either suspect at the exclusion of all others.

bond and was released. Smith returned to his job at a fast food restaurant and stated that he was innocent. Attorney McDougald indicated that he was planning to file a motion for dismissal of the case. Apparently McDougald was successful as court records show no record that Smith was ever indicted, according to Superior Court Clerk Joe Wilder. Wilder reviewed all grand jury records from 1986 to 1990 and found no indictment against Smith.

Task Force formed to continue investigation

At this point it appeared that the law enforcement authorities had struck out in their attempt to identify a legitimate suspect; however, a task force was created in July 1986 to continue the investigation. The task force comprised:

-Police Department Investigators Trawick and Stripling
-Sheriff Johnnie Becham
-Chief Deputy Sheriff Jimmy Jones
-Sheriff's Department Investigator Terry Deese
-GBI Agent Jack White of the Perry office
-District Attorney Willis Sparks
-Assistant District Attorney Wayne "Biff" Tillis

Leesburg convenience store assault case similar

GBI agent R. A. Smith and Chief Deputy Sheriff Jimmy Jones contacted Investigator Jerry Bowyer of the Lee County Sheriff's Office in Leesburg, Georgia, on February 20, 1986, about a similar assault case. Investigator Bowyer stated that a robbery and assault had occurred at Mr. B's convenience store outside Leesburg on January 27, 1986, at approximately 11:30 a.m. Officer Bowyer stated that the white female victim, Jill Spier, had been beaten with a hammer, which the black male assailant brought into the store concealed inside his jacket. The attack was without provocation—the clerk followed the assailant's instructions and said nothing to him that would have precipitated the attack. After instructing the clerk to lie on the floor, the black male started beating her on the back of the head. Following multiple blows, the clerk began to bleed very badly. She was wise enough, however, to lie very still after the assault. The assailant apparently assumed she was dead. Investigator Bowyer stated that the victim's life was spared because she covered the back of her head with her hands. Although her fingers were crushed and she sustained skull injuries, she survived the attack. A witness saw the black male exit from a brown Mustang. The attacker had been seen inside the store once before the attack when several merchandise vendors were present. Stolen was $291.93. Fingerprints were lifted from the cash register as evidence. The case remained unsolved at the time of the report.

Profile of Murderer

The National Center for the Analysis of Violent Crime (NCAVC) at the FBI Academy in Quantico, Virginia, rendered a criminal personality profile (Case Nr. 252-346, released in May 1986) of the person who killed Denise Allison. Preparers of the report were Police Investigative Profiler William Bradway, Special Agent W. Hagmaier, and Dr. James L. Luke. M. D.

GBI Special Agent Allen Smith provided subject report to Assistant District W. G. "Biff" Tillis on May 16, 1986.

Key points brought out in the report were:

The victim probably handed the bills to the perpetrator. This person then possibly decided that he wanted more than the money and in doing so met with resistance from the victim. The victim may have picked up a hammer (known to be kept near the cash register) for her defense and retreated toward the bathroom, possibly due to the fact that the front door exit was blocked by the killer or an associate. She also hoped that the bathroom was a safe haven if she could get the door shut or locked. The defensive wounds to the hands were most likely caused by the assailant's knife and were delivered in the bathroom. The blood on the walls and the commode were the result of these wounds.

The potato hoe became a weapon after the knife was broken during the scuffle in the bathroom. The victim, attempting to flee, was continuously struck by the killer using the hoe. The killer became frustrated by his lack of ability to control and dominate the victim and therefore continued swinging the hoe; but this instrument did not satisfy his lust for lethality so he resorted to the hammer, which was probably dropped in flight by the victim and rendered the final blows to her skull. The killer, then splattered with blood and in a state of panic, exited the store. He may have utilized victim's coat (missing) for the purpose of concealing the blood on his own clothing and person.

The killer, if he had accomplices, may have been deserted by them. It is possible one, acting as a look-out, observed the battle inside and retreated to a location where a vehicle was located. The witness (little boy playing in his backyard) may have observed this subject or the killer traveling through his yard.

The offender would most likely be a black male. The presence of Negroid hairs found in the victim's blood, the two previous robberies reportedly committed by a black male and also the racial makeup of the neighborhood all support the proposition that the killer would be black. The age of the killer is difficult to ascertain because of the wide variation of ages that commit these types of robberies. Statistically, however, we would propose that the killer's age would be late teens to late twenties. A consideration of the choice of weapons used to commit the crime (knife), which is indicative of a more youthful or inexperienced offender and the probable difficulty in procuring a handgun.

The killer apparently had a very difficult time in trying to control and dominate the victim. This probably was due to the consumption of alcohol, use of drugs, or the size and/or physical capabilities of the offender. If he had taken the victim's coat to conceal her blood, which his clothing was surely soiled by, it may have fit him. It is possible that he may have been involved in celebrating New Year's Eve, observed the lone female and tried to execute what appears to be a poorly planned spur-of-the-moment type robbery.

We would expect the killer to have a criminal history of "small-time" robberies (especially victimizing more vulnerable young and old victims), larcenies (displaying little or no sophistication), shoplifting and assaults. Any criminal record may also reflect reports of domestic assaults or disturbances. His history would also include some alcohol and/or drug abuse.

His friends and acquaintances would regard him as being quick-tempered and explosive. He is one that gets in the "first punch" and, because of his explosive behavior, does not have close friends. He would be described as forward and abusive toward women, especially younger ones he can intimidate.

If he is employed, it would be in a low-skilled job requiring manual labor. He would probably change jobs often. His education level would be less than high school and would reflect behavior problems while in school. We would expect that he depends upon others for living quarters. This could be family or friends that he draws from or he lives in subsidized housing. He probably relies on public transportation, acquaintances, or, if he possesses a vehicle, it would probably be an older model in poor repair.

He is familiar with the area of the homicide and either lives or frequents the vicinity. If he had been in the military service, we would expect he would serve in the ground forces; any discharge would be less than honorable, probably unsuitable in nature.

We would expect the killer to either secret himself in a safe haven or leave the area soon after the homicide. He would monitor media coverage until he is confident that the thrust of the investigation is not directed towards him and then he may resurface.

Immediately following the homicide, the killer would have sought a safe haven to remove the blood on him. We would expect him to wash his clothing and retain it unless the stains were too large. The victim's coat, if not stained too badly, may have been given to a female friend (of the perpetrator) who will probably still have custody of it. The stains would likely be on the inside.

Twenty years later, the murder remains unsolved

In summary, two men were arrested and charged with murder, but both were ultimately released due to insufficient evidence to support prosecution. Over twenty years later, the murder of Denise Allison–the most brutal and savage assault in Peach County history–remains unsolved and unprosecuted.

Forensic evidence still available

The crime lab in Atlanta returned to the Fort Valley Police Department all physical evidence collected at the crime scene and from individuals. The new Fort Valley Police Chief, John Anderson, has inventoried the evidence, including the claw hammer, potato hoe, and knife, and found that it is still available for DNA and other more sophisticated testing that was not possible back in 1986.

Court system let victim down, says Trawick

Detective Captain Gary Trawick, now retired, stated, "Win or lose, they should have given Denise Allison her day in court; she paid her life for that opportunity." Trawick added, "When I ride by

Denise's grave in Oaklawn Cemetery, tears always stream down my cheeks. As I stand beside her grave, I say, 'Denise, I tried but the court system let you down.' "

Sources:
- Fort Valley Police Department Case File: 13-0248-01-86 *
- Preliminary Hearing: State of Georgia vs. Ronnie Smith on charge of murder*
- *Leader Tribune* newspaper accounts
- Interviews with former and current law enforcement officers and officials
- Interviews with Denise Allison's family members

*Obtained through open records request.

This documentary of Denise Allison's murder is based solely on police and court records obtained through an open records request and is a factual account of the information gleaned from the case file. No inferences, opinions, or conclusions have been injected.

.

Chapter 12
Buried Alive in a Well:
the Saga of Nimrod Jackson

Nimrod Jackson:
renowned railroad worker at Byron's Flag Stop

When the Southwestern Railroad was completed from Macon to Fort Valley in 1851, locomotives coming from Macon took on wood at Byron and water at Powersville. The station at Echeeconee was designated number 1, Byron's flag stop was number one and a half, and Powersville was number 2. During the early 1890s, a young man named Nimrod Jackson, born (circa 1845) into slavery, took the job of supplying the wood rack and helping load wood on the trains that stopped at station one and a half. He was such a friendly, outgoing individual, and did his job so thoroughly and cheerfully, that railroad officials and employees praised his efforts and spoke of him in endearing tones.

Nimrod Jackson as envisioned in 1910.

The Old Devil Will Get You

When Nimrod Jackson was in his mid-sixties, he was engaged in digging and repairing wells. On Tuesday, April 5, 1910, Nimrod was working in a well on the farm of John Green Avera, the grandfather of Loren Arnold. He was sitting on a board that lay across the bucket with his legs wrapped around the rope. Nimrod had been lowered sixty-five feet down into the ninety-foot well by Charley Wilder (brother of Seaborn Wilder and father of Estelle Hallman), whose family lived in the house that used the well. Charlie's job was to raise or lower Nimrod with a windlass and to pass materials down to him as he needed them. Nimrod was removing the old curbing and installing new braces one board at a time without letting the loose earth crumble down. He was hammering at the boards and making a great racket, so loud that Ol' Charlie hollered down in jest, saying "You better cut out that noise, Nim. The old devil will get you if he hears you hammering at his door." At that moment fresh dirt started breaking loose, squeezing the curbing from all sides, and catching Nimrod's feet between the planks so he could not free them. The curbing above held, but Nimrod's legs were hopelessly trapped. Nimrod had a cool head and didn't panic. He simply asked Charlie to pull him out. When Charlie couldn't, Nimrod told him to go for help. Charlie spiked the windlass to secure Nimrod and ran for help.

The 6-Day Rescue Effort Begins

Everybody liked ol' Nim. He was a leader among his people and a favorite with the white children. Within an hour, dozens of men had gathered to offer their services. Not knowing whether the bottom twenty-five feet of the well had filled with dirt, men were lowered cautiously into the well to dig around Nimrod and to release his legs from the pressing boards. Every time they pried the boards, new volumes of sand would fall around them. Nimrod was covered to his shoulders several times and had to be dug out.

Wouldn't Take a Drink of Whisky

Jackson remained in good spirits as the rescue attempt proceeded. By day two, a large crowd had gathered to help free Nimrod. Women brought food, and he was fed regularly, but as time wore on he began to eat sparingly. An extra coat was sent down to keep him warm in the chilly depths. Nimrod had a reputation of being a heavy drinker at times, but he refused to accept a drink of whisky that was offered to him, even though a doctor advised him to drink it to guard against pneumonia. Nimrod felt too close to his Maker to imbibe. Nimrod always answered cheerfully that he was comfortable but stated he "sure would like to get out."

As Sunday rolled around, five days after the cave-in, the rescuers decided to dig a parallel well beside the old one. With two men digging and several others using the windlass to haul up buckets of dirt, the well descended at an astonishing rate of six feet per hour. By this time, more than a thousand people had begun a vigil at the well to watch the rescue operations.

Buried Alive

On the sixth day, around ten on Monday morning, the new well reached Nimrod's level. The men had planned to dig across to the old well, pull Nimrod out, and raise him back to safety. Suddenly, the unexpected happened, fresh sand began cascading around him. Nimrod could read the signs of the approaching end, for he cried out: "Farewell old world, farewell." At that instant, the dirt walls above him completely collapsed and eight feet of sand piled on top of him. The force of earth movement was so great that it buckled the wooden supports inside the new well like a rainbow. At this point, there was nothing the rescuers could do. Nimrod was hopelessly buried alive.

Mr. Green Avera, owner of the property, suggested they consult county officials before making any further efforts to dig up the body. The Superior Court was in session, so Mr. Avera asked Judge W. H. Felton what should be done about retrieving Nimrod's remains. Judge Felton decided that the risk would be too great to attempt to recover the body, so he ordered that the well be filled and that Nimrod remain buried there. Nimrod has been buried there for nearly a hundred years.

Spectators Came From Miles Around

Thousands of people flocked to the well to witness the rescue work, some coming from as far as seventy-five to one-hundred miles. During the six-day ordeal, an estimated four thousand people visited the site. Nearly one hundred automobiles made the journey and there's no telling how many wagons. The well had to be roped off so the rescuers could work without spectator interference.

Another important event occurred that week: Warren Seaborn Wilder was born in the farm house that used the well. So everyone who came inquired about the health of the baby and the welfare of the mother. As Nimrod was leaving this world, another young life was entering it. Warren Seaborn Wilder had three younger sisters: Inez Wilder Ellis of Perry, Georgia; Una Wilder

Martin of Perry, Georgia; and Lucy Wilder Talton of Kathleen, Georgia, and one brother, Harold, now deceased.

Nimrod's Ghost

Many in the farming community believed in ghosts and would not venture near the well site after sundown. After the well had been filled with dirt, a sinkhole appeared atop the old well about two feet across and three feet deep. It was believed that Nimrod's ghost came out of the well, leaving a depression in the sand.

Seaborn Wilder, the father of the infant Warren Seaborn Wilder, had covered the depression over Nimrod's grave with loose boards. Unbeknownst to Wilder, one of his hens had made a nest beneath the boards. One evening as the sun disappeared over the horizon and the shadows of night crept in, Wilder was standing with his back to the old well. He inadvertently stepped backwards on the boards and in the process crushed the hen. Out came the hen in the dead of night fluttering and flapping wildly around his head and squawking loudly. Wilder thought it was Nimrod's ghost. It frightened him so badly that he ran into a tree trying to flee. It was quite a while before Wilder's nerves settled down.

House by the well

Loren Arnold of Fort Valley, Georgia, grew up in the house (burned down during the 1950s) that sat next to the well where Nimrod was buried alive. "When I was in grammar school, the well site was only thirty-five to forty yards from my bedroom window," stated Loren. "It was a spooky place. When my brother, James Jr., and I started cutting up at nighttime, mother would make us leave the house and walk around the old well site in the dark...that cured us from misbehaving."

Folklore has it that on a quiet night you can hear Nimrod hammering down in the well. You can rest assured of one thing; you won't catch me out there after dark!

The search for the old well site

Although the legend of Nimrod Jackson had passed from generation to generation, no one seemed to know the location of the well wherein Nimrod Jackson perished nearly a hundred years ago. This piqued my interest, so, in December 2004, I set out to find the old well. After inquiring throughout the community, by a chance encounter I ran into Steve Hancock, whose grandfather had told him about Nimrod Jackson. Steve stated that the well was located on the section of the Hancock farm owned by Charles "Chuck" Hancock, which was farmed by Steve and his father, George. After making an appointment with Steve to meet him at the site on January 18, 2005, I picked up Fred Shepard and Judge George Culpepper, and we drove out to the Hancock Farm, where we were met by Steve and George Hancock. Steve had driven a stake in the ground to mark the exact location of the well. Steve stated that his grandfather, R. T. Hancock Sr., twenty-one years old at the time, came from Lizella, Georgia, to the Avera farm to witness the rescue efforts. "Grandfather told me there were worlds of people here," stated Steve. Steve stated that the depression over the former well remained noticeable for many years until the land was cleared and plowed over. George Hancock advised that his father, R. T. Hancock Sr., bought Green Avera's farm in 1941 from Ethel Avera Arnold, the daughter of farm owner Green Avera and mother of Loren Arnold of Fort Valley.

L-R: Fred Shepard, George Hancock, Steve Hancock, and Judge George Culpepper stand at the former well site on the Hancock Farm where the fatal cave-in occurred.

Campaign kicked off to fund memorial for Nimrod

Since Nimrod's gravesite was not marked, both Fred Shepard and Judge Culpepper wondered if Nimrod ever received a funeral. After Nimrod's family confirmed that he did not have a funeral, this author, through the local *Leader Tribune* newspaper, began a campaign to raise money to purchase a memorial and provide a funeral for Nimrod, an effort fully supported by its editor, Vicky Davis. Over fifteen hundred dollars was raised from private contributors. A grave maker was purchased from Clark Memorials in Macon. Jimmy Duke graciously contributed a black wrought iron fence to border the gravesite and oversaw the preparation of the gravesite including concreting its base, installing the fence, and positioning the grave marker. Dennis Herbert engraved, without charge, a plaque summarizing the life of Nimrod Jackson that would be attached to the fence. Rooks

99

Funeral Home and Edwards Funeral Home, both of Fort Valley, provided tents, chairs, and voice amplification equipment. Rev. Dennis Stalvey helped design the program for the funeral service and printed over five hundred copies on quality paper. Larry Smith Florist of Fort Valley provided a beautiful floral arrangement with an eternal light attached thereto that would glow at night. JCH Video Productions of Fort Valley filmed the event for posterity. A Blue Grass band from the Powersville Opry House provided the music: Blanton "Bill" Redding, Everett Clackler, Mike Koester, and Rev. Roland Everett Fall. Television stations, newspapers, and radio stations covered the event.

The service was held on Saturday, June 4, 2005, with four ministers officiating: two African-American ministers (Reverend Nathaniel Ross, pastor, Saint Louis CME Church, Fort Valley; and Rev. Curtis West, pastor, Bethel CME Church, Macon, Georgia, who preached the service) and two white ministers (Rev. Dennis Stalvey, pastor, Fort Valley United Methodist Church and Roland Everett Fall, Associate Pastor of the Perry United Methodist Church). Rev. Fall was so moved by the legend of Nimrod Jackson that he wrote a ballad concerning Nimrod's life. At the service, Rev. Fall sang and played the "Ballad of Nimrod Jackson" to the accompaniment of the Blue Grass band.

Ballad of Nimrod Jackson
By Rev. Roland Everett Fall

Many years have come and gone since 1892,
When a freed man was hired to work the trains and keep
them on their way,
His name was Nimrod Jackson, he pitched fuel wood
on the train,
Oiled the mighty engines, checked the brakes, and checked
the chains,

At station one and a half between Echeeconee and Powersville,
Nimrod Jackson distinguished himself for the job he did so well,
His work was highly regarded, the engineers all knew his name,
Ol' Nim, they said, was the best there was keeping the
Georgia trains,
Chorus
Living his life day by day, giving all that he had,
Nimrod Jackson made his way down the road to the
promised land,
He said his Maker would provide if he would do his best,
Ol' Nim never wavered in that way through life's many a test,

Later in life at age 65 Ol' Nim was still working hard,
He had learned to dig and repair old wells, he worked on
*   many a farm,*
With skill he dug through the Georgia clay, bringing
*   water to dry, thirsty land,*
He was deep in a well one April day he heard an awful sound,

He heard the well boards bow and break and sand come
*   rushing in,*
His legs were trapped sixty feet underground, against
*   the sidewall he was pinned,*
He called to the ropeman, "Pull me out!" but he couldn't
*   pull him up,*
"Go for help!" Ol' Nim said, "Maybe you can get me out,"

Chorus
Many came to help that day, they tried hard to bring relief,
They went to work on a parallel well, and almost got that deep,
But suddenly the walls they shook and the boards began to break,
The walls caved in, Ol' Nim was lost and the well became
*   his grave,*

For six long days they'd dug and prayed, but Ol' Nim could
*   not be saved,*
"Farewell, old world, farewell!" he said, as the dirt
*   walls gave way,*
On the farm where the well took ol'Nim's life, a baby was
*   born that week,*
As one life departed another began with a baby's cry so sweet.

Over five hundred people attended. Nimrod's relatives came from far and wide, and Peach Countians turned out in record numbers. It was an emotional time as both races bonded together to pay tribute to a folk hero of another time and to praise a former Civil War slave whose actions and deeds had earned him the respect and admiration of his community. The descendants of Nimrod Jackson came away teary-eyed, yet contented in spirit for they experienced fulfillment in celebrating Nimrod's life and felt a sense of

The Rev. Roland Everett Fall sings and plays ballad.

101

closure in knowing he had finally received a proper funeral.

Nimrod Jackson's grave. Birth: Circa 1845. Death: April 11, 1910. The epitaph chosen by his family were Nimrod's final words: "Farewell old world, farewell." Wording of the plaque attached to fence reads:

"Nimrod Jackson was a Peach County legend. He was born into slavery and survived the Civil War. Around 1890 he came by train from Virginia to Byron with his wife, Jane, and six children. He distinguished himself as an outstanding railroad worker at Jackson Station and as a well digger. He perished in a well cave-in at this site in April 1910. Crews worked around-the-clock for six days to rescue him, but a final cave-in sealed his fate. He was a leader among his people and loved by both races. This child of God, buried 65 feet below, awaits the mighty trumpet call of God when the dead in Christ shall rise to forever be with the Lord.

Great-great-granddaughter Yolanda Thornton (right) and other family members place flowers on Nimrod Jackson's grave. Photo Courtesy: Danny Gilleland

Author Billy Powell and Hattie Lewis Gray, Nimrod Jackson's only living granddaughter, at Nimrod's funeral. Photo Courtesy: Danny Gilleland.

There were "two" Nimrod Jacksons

What are the odds of there being two Nimrod Jacksons who lived in the Byron area during the nineteenth century: one, a black man, and the other, a white man, and both being responsible for maintaining the wood rack at the railroad flag stop called Jackson Station? Bill Boyd wrote in the *Macon Telegraph* during the 1980s that the railroad flag stop at Byron was named Jackson Station after the "black" Nimrod Jackson. Unaware there was another individual named Nimrod Jackson, this writer initially was led to believe that the flag stop was named after the "black" Nimrod. In response, however, Byron historians Betsy Peavy Murdock and Jackie Edwards strongly contended that Jackson Station was not named after the "black" Nimrod, but was named after a "white" man also named Nimrod Jackson.

Family Tree and descendants of the black Nimrod Jackson

Nimrod Jackson, born circa 1845 and died in 1910, and his wife, Jane, had seven children: three sons (Shula, Walter, and Henry) and four daughters (Classic Mae, Nettie, Stella, and Rosa).

The great-grandchildren of this Nimrod Jackson, who reside in Fort Valley, Byron, and Macon, say that Nimrod Jackson, his wife, Jane, and six children (son Henry did not accompany family) came here from Virginia by freight train (as hobos) and got off the train at Bateman, the former name of Byron. Nimrod, a survivor of the Civil War, was seeking employment opportunities in the Deep South after the Reconstruction era. His primary occupation was working for the railroad at the Byron flag stop and his secondary employment was digging and repairing wells. The foregoing information is based on the testimony of Rosa Jackson Lewis, the youngest of Nimrod's seven children.

Rosa Jackson (1887-1950) married Ed Lewis. This union produced fifteen children of which Hattie Lewis Gray of Lithonia, Georgia, was number thirteen. Hattie has two daughters: Virginia Culbreath and Constance Rutledge, both living in the greater Atlanta area. Both Culbreath and Rutledge are great-granddaughters of Nimrod Jackson and occupy the same kinship in the Jackson family tree as Eugene Fluellen Jr., Mary Fluellen Oates, Annie Rumph Stubbs, Rosetta Rumph Smith, Eddie Fluellen, and Hattie Ruth Simmons (now deceased) all of Fort Valley, and Jerry Rumph from Macon.

Virginia Culbreath has a daughter, Yolanda Culbreath Thornton, from Lithonia, Georgia, who is a great-great-granddaughter of Nimrod. The newest great-great-great-grandson of Nimrod Jackson is Bryce Thornton, the son of Paul and Yolanda Thornton, born in February 2006. There are many other descendants of Nimrod Jackson, too many to mention in this chapter.

Hattie Lewis Gray of Lithonia, Georgia, the only living granddaughter of Nimrod, provided additional family information: (1) Nimrod's wife, Jane, died before Nimrod perished in the well in 1910. Nimrod's youngest daughter, Rosa Jackson, was with her mother during Jane's last hours. Nimrod was at work when Jane passed. (2) Since there was no surviving spouse to handle the arrangements, Nimrod never received a funeral. (3 Nimrod's youngest child, Rosa Jackson, visited the well site many times after her father's death. Honey bees had built a beehive at the well. (4) After Jane Jackson died, Nimrod moved from Byron to Macon and lived in the Vineville area. (5) Nimrod's eldest son, Henry, who did not make the trip with the family from Virginia to Byron circa 1890, later established himself in Jersey City, New Jersey. (6) Two elder sisters of Rosa Jackson later settled in Jersey City also. (8)

Hattie's deceased baby sister, Teresa Ross, has daughters—also Nimrod's great-grandchildren—living in and around Fort Valley, Georgia.

Nimrod Jackson's great-grandchildren whose grandmother was Rosa Jackson Lewis: L-R: Jerry Rumph of Macon, Georgia; Annie Rumph Stubbs, Mary Fluellen Oates, and Eugene Fluellen Jr., all from Fort Valley. Eugene was the former chief of Security at Fort Valley State University.

Visiting the grave of Rosa Jackson Lewis, 1887-1950, youngest daughter of Nimrod Jackson (in cemetery behind Blue Bird Body Company) were Rosa's grandson Eugene Fluellen (R) with his grandchildren, L-R: Selena, Alexandria, and Eric.

105

Family tree and Descendants of the white Nimrod Jackson

Betsy Peavy Murdock, a great-great-great-granddaughter of the white Nimrod Jackson, provided the following documentation verifying his existence and supporting her contention that the Byron flag stop was named after him: (1) He was born October 22, 1795, in the Orangeburg district of South Carolina. (2) He married Elizabeth Busbee in 1814 and they settled initially in Crawford County. (3) They had twelve children: Parmelia, Martha, Felder, Mitta, Ebenezer, Eliza, William, Elizabeth, John, Rabun, Perry, and Green. (4) Descendants of Felder, Ebenezer, and Elizabeth live in the Byron area. (5) Nimrod was a property owner of substance and owned land along the railroad. (6) Nimrod was a great hunter, who hunted with the Indians, particularly Chief William McIntosh. Legend has it that Nimrod acquired land from the Indians in exchange for a cow and a calf. (7) At the flag stop (initially called "Number One and One-Half Station"), he provided a wood rack and supplied wood for the

Descendants of the white Nimrod Jackson: Kneeling L-R: Ben Groce, Victoria Klinger, Julia Peavy, Konner Allred. Seated L-R: Ben Robertson, Mary Shipman, Ruby Allred, Betsy Murdock, Bill Robertson, Joe Thames. Standing third low, L-R: Cathy Groce, Ashley Groce, Jackie Brown, James Allred, Jay Allred holding Will Allred, Kaleb Allred, Karen Thames. Last row, L-R: Hannah Groce, Marie Simar, Wright Peavy, Russell Jones, Tony Allred, Bucky Green. Not pictured is Ronnie Collier from Perry, Georgia.

steam engines. (8) The Southwestern Railroad named the flag stop "Jackson Station" after Mr. Jackson, probably during the 1850s. (9) Nimrod died October 15, 1866, in Crawford County. (10) He is buried on Hartley Bridge Road between Byron and the Boy Scout Camp, nearer to the camp than town. (11) There are nineteen known descendants in the Byron area, one of whom was Christine Jackson Thames Green, a great-granddaughter, now deceased, who kept genealogical records on the Jackson family for many years.

Which Nimrod was Jackson Station named after?

The "white" Nimrod Jackson had already been living in the area for approximately thirty-two years when the railroad reached Byron around 1846. The "black" Nimrod Jackson arrived in Byron around 1890-1892. This time frame is based on the fact his youngest child, Rosa, died in 1950 at the age of sixty-three, placing her birth in 1887. Estimating that Rosa was three to five years old when her family came to Byron places the arrival date between 1890 and 1892.

The preponderance of the evidence points toward the flag stop being named after the "white" Nimrod Jackson, who had been dead some twenty-four to twenty-six years before the "black" Nimrod Jackson arrived in Byron. He was also a man of means and influence and the most logical choice.

Both Nimrod Jacksons, however, rank among Peach County's most historic personalities during the nineteenth century. The "black" Nimrod Jackson worked at Jackson Station and was the top well digger in the area. He was a leader among his people, well respected by both races, and loved by all children. The "white" Nimrod Jackson, one of Byron's earliest pioneers, made significant contributions to the railroad and the Byron community and has many descendants living in the area.

The old well where the "black" Nimrod is buried was located, but the gravesite of the "white" Nimrod has never been found, although several searches have been made by his descendants. The most amazing thing about this story is how a white man and a black man both had such an unusual name and both worked at Jackson Station.

Directions to Nimrod's Grave

Turn off Moseley Road (Old Macon Road) onto Mathews Store Road and proceed to the point where it dead-ends. Take a left onto East Wesley Chapel Road and go approximately two-tenths of a mile. Enter at the gate on east side of road. Nimrod's grave, surrounded by a metal fence, is located about one hundred yards from the road and behind a pecan grove.

Sources: *Atlanta Journal*
     Macon Telegraph
     Leader Tribune
     Nimrod Jackson family records
     Interviews with members of Wilder family, Hancock family,
      and Loren Arnold

Chapter 13
Man Buried Crossways the World

Not far from the Peach County line resides the little hamlet of Oglethorpe, Georgia, whose cemetery offers a most unusual attraction. On Colonel Fish Avenue in the cemetery near a large magnolia tree is the unmarked grave of a man who is buried crossways – his grave is facing north to south instead of the traditional west to east direction. His name is Jim Loyd. He was hung in 1872 for being an accomplice in the murder of Colonel George W. Fish, a district court judge and prominent Oglethorpe citizen. Loyd requested he be buried only in an undershirt, with no buttons, and a sheet wrapped around his waist and lower body. Further, he asked to be buried north to south, saying he had always lived "crossways with the world."

Jim Loyd's best friend was John Holsenback. They lived together in Oglethorpe. Holsenback confided to Loyd that Colonel Fish had grievously wronged him. Loyd advised Holsenback to kill Judge Fish. Consequently, they conspired together and devised a plan to kill Fish with his own gun. Knowing that Fish's gun was in the repair shop, Loyd begged the proprietor to let him borrow it to shoot squirrels, promising to return it before Colonel Fish would call for it. Loyd stuffed the gun's muzzle with special wadding. The opportunity presented itself one afternoon in the spring of 1871 when Col. Fish left on the train for Macon. Knowing Fish would return late that night, Holsenback hid in the doorway of the old courthouse (same building that later housed Taylor's pharmacy and now Jon Coogle's law office). After Fish got off the train, he walked toward the middle of town. As Fish approached the courthouse, Holsenback bolted out the side door (the one facing Highway 49) and fatally shot Col. Fish in the dark of night. He slipped away unseen.

Finding a dead body on the street the next morning, Oglethorpe residents were abuzz with excitement. To deflect suspicion, Holsenback requested a coroner's jury investigate the murder. After the coroner ruled it a homicide, Holsenback followed the body to the Fish home (at that time, located across street from J. H. Taylor's present home). He helped carry the corpse, tenderly placing Col. Fish in the casket. Unexpectedly, Mrs. Fish knelt at the side of the casket, and prayed the assassin might come forward and touch her husband's face. Momentarily unnerved, Holsenback fought to control his composure, and hastily left the house.

Governor Rufus Bullock, a friend of Fish, sent two detectives, Rasberry and Murphy, to solve the crime. After their investigation, Holsenback and Loyd were arrested on suspicion of murder and jailed. The two detectives hid inside a large, wooden washstand positioned with the open end facing the wall in Holsenback and Loyd's cell. Throughout the night the detectives heard the suspects discuss the details of the shooting.

The two men were charged with murder and a trial held on June 28, 1871, at the Oglethorpe courthouse (across the street from the present courthouse). It was the most sensational trial ever conducted in Macon County. A capacity crowd heard Jim Loyd speak for three hours. His lawyer tried to stop his outrageous testimony, but couldn't. Judge Clark requested those in the courtroom never to divulge what Loyd said.

Both Holsenback and Loyd received the death sentence and remained in the Oglethorpe jail while their lawyers requested a new trial. Loyd walked the jail floor until the nails in the floor were shiny. Holsenback chiseled through the brick wall and made a getaway, but didn't get very far. The prisoners were then taken to Albany for safe-keeping.

The day before the execution, Holsenback and Loyd were returned from Albany by train, guarded by fifty men. Sheriff Red Hill resigned, saying he could not hang his friend's son. A tremendous crowd converged on Oglethorpe for the hanging, even a flatcar of people from Marshallville. Spectators positioned themselves in trees and on roof tops. A carnival atmosphere prevailed. Max Styles, an entrepreneur, sold water for five cents a glass. Loyd acted like a buffoon. Riding in a buggy from the train to the gallows, Loyd talked incessantly, clapped his hands, and wouldn't allow anyone to pray for him. When Loyd reached the gallows, he calmly sat on the steps and, chewing a wad of tobacco, spat tobacco juice on his own coffin. Allowed to speak before his hanging, he denounced everything and everyone in Oglethorpe.

Violet Moore, the renowned writer and poet from Macon County, published a poem entitled: "Crossways with the World." Mrs. Moore, in the couplets below, described Jim Loyd's verbal attack on Oglethorpe citizens, including his unusual burial request:

He stood in court so pale and gaunt
    That final, fatal day
"Your honor, you are hanging me
    Now let me have my say!"

They say that John talked for hours
    The secrets of the town
Were spread out for the world to see
    When handsome John sat down.

The women groaned, the pastor moaned
    The men were 'bout to riot,
At last the Judge stood tall and grim
    And ordered John, "Be quiet!"

"Just one more word, let my poor bones
    "In just a sheet be furled
"And have me buried North to South
    "At crossways with the world."

"For crossways with the world I've lived
    "And crossways I must die..."

John Holsenback was reserved; however, his estranged wife, also the Oglethorpe postmistress, seemed cheerful. She even asked some children passing by if they were going to the "neck stretching." She watched the hanging from the attic of the old Eagle and Phoenix Hotel. Gus Lee, the executioner from Marshallville, fainted after dropping the platform and seeing the men dangling from their nooses. Mrs. Loyd also fainted. Jim Loyd died instantly. John Holsenback's neck was not broken, but he slowly choked to death.

Several days before the execution, Lucy and Tom Loyd, children of the condemned man, journeyed to Milledgeville and begged Governor James Smith to pardon their father, but the governor refused. After the hanging, Jim Loyd's wife became indignant. She walked up and down the road praying the earth would open and swallow up Macon County and everything in it. She also prayed that Gus Lee and Governor Smith would burn in hell. Jim Loyd was buried in Oglethorpe's cemetery. John Holsenback's remains were transported to Columbia County for burial.

Jim Loyd's grave faces north to south and perpendicular to other graves in cemetery.

The ghost of Colonel Fish lived on and routinely haunted the old Fish home. M. L. Shealy bought the house from Fish's widow in 1872. Ninety years later, in 1962, Mr. and Mrs. Donald Nelson purchased the house. In 1969, the Nelsons moved it to Americus. No one dared sit in Col. Fish's velvet chair in the front parlor, where his disapproving presence was felt. Dr. Nelson reportedly had a conversation with the apparition of Col. Fish, who was upset his house had been moved to Americus.

In 1971, Dr. and Mrs. Gatewood Dudley purchased the home from their friends, the Nelsons, and began restoration of the old house, built by Fish in 1852. (When Fish built his house during the 1850s, Oglethorpe was a railroad boom town with a population of 15,000 and missed becoming the state capitol by only one vote.) Whereas Colonel Fish's ghost became angry and restive after the Nelsons moved the house, his ghost seemed pleased with the Dudley's restoration project, which involved an infusion of eighteenth century furniture from England with valuable family heirlooms. To this day, Colonel Fish's ghost still roams the old house, and one asymmetrical grave in Oglethorpe's cemetery testifies of a sensational, yet tragic chronicle in Macon County's history.

Sources: *History of Macon County, Georgia*
                 Atlanta Journal and Constitution Magazine, April 29, 1973

Chapter 14
Bliss, Sylvan Dell, and Dope Hill

Where were Bliss, Sylvan Dell, and Dope Hill?

Since moving to Fort Valley in 1959, I overheard people from time-to-time refer to a magical place called "Bliss." In the same breath, they would rattle off remembrances of "Sylvan Dell" and "Dope Hill." Since few citizens have knowledge of these three historic places, I decided to conduct research and share my findings. Jimmy Duke got things rolling by taking me in his truck and retracing the path of the old Macon Road. As he drove along, Jimmy pointed out the locations of Bliss, Sylvan Dell, and Dope Hill. Next, Wallis Hardeman, Fred Shepard, and I spent two hours driving slowly over the same route. I took notes as Fred and Wallis discussed landmarks.

Directions to Dope Hill, Sylvan Dell, and Bliss

1-Fred Shepard stated that construction of Highway 49 from Fort Valley to Byron was begun in 1934. It was completed in 1938, according to Henry Outler. The Highway 49 bridge is dated 1935, said Leonard Giles.

2-Consequently, from the early 1900s to 1934, the old Macon Road (a dirt road) was the principal route to Byron and

Picrtured at Dope Hill are L-R: Billy Marshall, Virgil Booker, Jimmy Duke, Marcus Hickson, Nick Strickland Jr. (his father operated the store there), and Buddy Luce.

Macon. The road started at Five Points and crossed Blue Bird's present parking lot (Blue Bird built in 1935). It then proceeded down a ravine (near the old cemetery) and rose to the top of the hill, called Dope Hill. Marcus Hickson stated that Jack Duke ran a sawmill down in that ravine. Buster Beck said that J. E. Bozeman's house was close to Blue Bird and that E. J. Saywell's Machine Shop was adjacent to Duke's sawmill.

3-Proceeding up Dope Hill and just around the curve was a country store that sat on the corner where Taylor's Mill Road intersected the old Macon Road. The store was just beyond the city limits in that day.

4-Continuing north is the county barn located across the road from the present city limit sign. Next is a railroad overpass, about one mile from the county barn. The overpass, a wooden bridge, was removed years ago for safety reasons. Wallis Hardeman said that the old Macon Road originally crossed the railroad at ground level. He reasoned that the potential for accidents prompted construction of the overpass. Billy Marshall and Henry Outler remember that Johns Dairy was across the railroad tracks from the old ice plant (still standing) and located in the vicinity of the present recycling center.

5- After driving three-tenths of a mile from the other side (north side) of overpass, Wallis and Fred had me stop the car. "On the right side of the road was Willie Joe Braswell's Dairy," said Wallis. "The land in this area and what is now Pine Needles Country Club was owned by the Braswells." Fred Shepard then observed, "And on the left side of the road sat the Peach Hotel where transient workers stayed during peach season." Wallis continued, "Braswell's

Fred Shepard (L) and Wallis Handeman (R) discuss historic landmarks.

Dairy delivered milk twice a day." Fred added, "My sister and I would fight over who got the cream."

6- Just beyond Ralph Champion's house and seven-tenths of a mile from the overpass is Alabama Street. Wallis remarked, "That was the old road to Sylvan Dell."

After passing Wilder Dent's home, we approached another railroad crossing—roughly 1.2 miles from the overpass where the railroad curves back and again crosses the old Macon Road. There you can see Sylvan Dell Road, which is four-tenths of a mile long from Highway 49 and dead-ends at the railroad crossing.

7-Continuing across the tracks we passed two houses, the last one being Don Hudson's. The old Macon Road stops in Don's yard due to the dense woods ahead.

8- A line drawn from Don Hudson's to Minyard's Garage marks the path of the old Macon Road. It exited just below Minyard's, crossed Highway 49 (which didn't exist then) to Moseley Road, and proceeded to Byron. The area between the second railroad crossing and Minyard's Garage is Bliss. At the center of Bliss was a wooden bridge that spanned Mossy Creek. Its great attraction was the swimming hole on the east side of the bridge.

9. Sylvan Dell was a picnic area located between present Highway 49 and Mississippi Clark's house at 101 Sylvan Dell Road (Linda Johnson lives there now). It featured an artesian well where cool water—with a sulfur taste—flowed from a three-inch pipe. This was a favorite gathering place for Peach Countians. Billy Marshall said that dating teenagers often used it as a parking spot.

Gristmills and Sawmills at Bliss

Braswell Mathew's grandfather once owned Bliss. Mathews is a renowned architect who restored the California state capitol building and accomplished many other architectural feats.

My first cousin, Robert Braswell Mathews, of Pacific Palisades, California, informed me that our great-great-great-grandfather, Williamson E. Mims (1787-1863), owned a fifteen-hundred acre plantation near Fort Valley that encompassed the area of Bliss. Cousins David Sammons and Dorothy Mathews Walker are equally kin to Mims. Mims owned eighty-two slaves and operated a gristmill and a sawmill there. His gristmill was located on Mossy Creek. Mims sold the right of way on his land to the Southwestern Railroad when the railroad was being constructed from Macon to Fort Valley. Mims is thought to have given Bliss its name.

Lee Posey gave me a Peach County map that still reflects Bliss. The Braswell family became connected with this property through Mims' daughter, Sara Anne, who married William Braswell. Mims willed three hundred acres of the plantation to his daughter. William and Sara Anne Mims Braswell lost two sons in the Battle of Atlanta: William and Samuel. Their third son, Robert (my great-grandfather), survived and settled in Fort Valley. He was the father of Willie Joe Braswell, who ran the dairy near Bliss.

Sylvan Dell

The picnic area and artesian spring were the major attractions at Sylvan Dell. Ernest Rumph said the three-inch pipe

was still standing forty-four years ago (1960) when he moved across from Mississippi Clark's house. "Fifteen years ago a tree fell and broke the pipe off," stated Rumph. "When the county laid water lines to Powersville, they ruptured a vein in the spring, causing it to flow underground and dry-up."

The spring was located west of Mississippi Clark's backyard and approximately seventy-five yards from the shoulder of Highway 49. Wallis Hardeman and Charles Evans went out to Sylvan Dell during 1980s. They noticed that the carved initials of teenagers were still visible on the trees. In 1926, when Fort Valley High School was built, Wallis and

Ernest and Betty Rumph at artesian spring site.

his classmates (Robert Thorpe, John A. Houser, George Anderson-sheriff's son, Edwin Haslem, and Peck Mathews) transplanted ten oak saplings from Sylvan Dell to the school grounds. Nearly eighty years later, large oak trees surround the old high school, bearing mute testimony to this deed.

Dope Hill

During the 1920s-1940s, a blue law prohibited the sale of Coca-Cola on Sunday. Bob Marchman said that Coca-Cola in those days contained trace amounts of cocaine. Southerners called it "Dope." To circumvent this law, a store just beyond the city limits sold Coca-Cola on Sunday. A steady stream of people would drive out there on Sundays to buy Coca-Cola. Originally made from fresh coca leaves, Coca-Cola is now made from denatured coca in which the cocaine has been removed. Wallis Hardeman stated that Henry

Hance owned the store. "I remember riding out there with my father after church to get a Coke," chuckled Wallis. Fred Shepard recalled that Nick Strickland Sr. once operated the store. "He gased up my car and put in a quart of oil," said Fred. "In those days, they didn't sell oil in cans. Nick went over to an oil drum, pumped the oil into a metal cup having a trigger, and then poured it into the crankcase." Fred continued, "It was a typical country store where they sold drinks, tobacco, crackers, and canned goods."

Significant Discovery: Old Bliss Bridge Found

I tracked Mossy Creek about one-quarter mile downstream from the present Highway 49 bridge and found remains of the old

Directly behind Billy Marshall stand the old pilings that once supported the old Macon Road bridge.

Macon Road bridge at Bliss still standing. The pilings have been there eighty to a hundred years. There, practically unchanged, was the famous swimming hole that old-timers remember with such joy.

More Remembrances of Bliss

Mrs. Martha Minyard Silas shared with this writer many wonderful memories of Bliss. Martha graduated from Fort Valley High School in 1936 and was the valedictorian of her class. She taught school for forty years at Glascock County, and is now retired and living in Warner Robins. Her parents were John and Johnnie Adams Minyard. Her brother was Horace Minyard and her sisters are Rosa Minyard Greer and Mary Ann Minyard Goss. Fred Shepard remembers going to school with Martha. "Martha was my friend and a sweet, intelligent, and pretty lady," said Fred.

Martha's parents bought a farm at Bliss in 1934. "The old Macon road, a dirt road then, was on one side of our dwelling," she stated. "When Highway 49 was paved, the dwelling faced the new highway. Before the construction of Highway 49, if you can imagine, there was no road whatsoever in front of the Minyard home place." Martha continued, "Bliss was well known in those days. It was even listed on the maps of land surveyors. Travelers on Greyhound buses only had to tell the driver to let him them off at Bliss, and the driver would stop right in front of the Minyard home."

Martha said that a favorite place to swim was near the old wooden bridge that spanned Mossy Creek: "Youth from Fort Valley and Byron would catch a ride to Bliss, and then walk down the dirt road to the swimming hole." Martha revealed that many people were baptized in Mossy Creek near the old bridge. "When Nellie Lee Giles and her husband Rayford Collins joined Wesley Chapel Methodist Church, they preferred immersion over sprinkling so they were baptized in Mossy Creek. When my dad and mother joined Wesley Chapel, they too were baptized there. Several black churches also baptized their converts at the old bridge. We could hear them singing from our house."

Martha added, "Leonard Giles was right about the Highway 49 bridge being built in 1935. That date was engraved on the bridge. Leonard was a little boy when the bridge was built and I was a teenager, but he always said I was his sweetheart."

Martha's mother wrote a poem about Bliss. Its first stanza reads:

'Tis a pleasant place
Where we the youngsters meet.
We splash, we dive
We have such fun.
'Tis a summer's treat.

Uncovering these three historic landmarks—Bliss, Sylvan Dell, and Dope Hill—was a most gratifying and thrilling experience. For a moment, we stepped back in time and re-captured an era in Peach County's storied past that will never be forgotten.

Chapter 15
Slappey's Opera House and Peach Theater

George Slappey Builds Theater

The old theater, located on South Main Street (fourth building from Herbert Jewelers), once occupied a special place in the lives of Fort Valleyans. It opened on January 3, 1917, with a reported 750 people attending the stage play *Peg of My Heart* performed by a traveling theater company. During the early 1970s, the theater closed with the movie *Help* starring the Beetles.

Those who enjoyed the old theatre can thank its builder, Mr. George Slappey (1871-1934). Mr. Slappey, originally a pharmacist, purchased a vacant downtown lot in 1901 and built a drug store— the same lot where the theater now stands. Slappey couldn't resist the lure of riches in the peach industry and made a fortune growing and shipping peaches. Since he was once a druggist, many called him "Dr. Slappey." When Slappey's vision of a theater came to fruition, he instructed his architect to construct it with "the sumptuousness of a palace, the convenience of a house, and the agreeableness of a county seat."

Judge Bryant Culpepper, chairman of Fort Valley's Downtown Development Authority and Main Street program, stated that the original Slappey Opera House and stage were located on the second floor. On the third floor was a spectator balcony overlooking the stage. The ground floor housed R.S. Braswell & Sons, one of the finest dry goods stores in the region. R.S. Braswell, my great uncle, advertised exten-

Superior Court Judge Bryant Culpepper, Chairman of the Fort Valley DDA, describes how theater facade will be restored to orginal appearance.

sively in the *Leader Tribune*. George Slappey named his creation the Austin Theater after his good friend, Samuel " Bully" Austin, the son of local physician, Dr. David Austin (1817-1879), and his wife, Emily Braswell, (my great-great-aunt). At the time, Bully Austin was editor of the local newspaper, *The Leader.*

Mr. Slappey loaned the theater out for community activities, such as a Fiddler's Convention, to raise money for charity. The Slappey building was the first to install ground-level lights to illuminate the sidewalk and front of building. The structure also served as Peach County's Courthouse in 1925 with Judge Henry Mathews presiding.

Mr. Slappey had no children. His first wife was Fannie Harris (1873-1893), daughter of H.C. Harris, owner of the old Winona Hotel. His second wife was Clara Visscher, a beautiful lady, according to historical records. Thomas Flournoy's history reveals that in Clara's delirium, before her death in 1919, she admitted to indiscretions, so Slappey never marked her grave. His third wife was Eva Kavannaugh. Slappey, during the late 1920s, built a cabin named "Sleepy Hollow" between Fort Valley and Marshallville with a large ballroom where he held parties and dances during the weekends.

Newspapers Chronicle Theater Opening:

- *The Leader Tribune, June 9, 1916:* "Mr. George Slappey is going to give Fort Valley one of its finest dry goods stores in the state. Over the floor will be an up-to-date auditorium. The work of remodeling the store formerly owned by John B. Vance started last week. It will be completed by September 1, costing over $8000."

- *Perry's Home Journal, Jan 3, 1917:* "Delegations of people from Montezuma, Perry, Marshallville, and other towns attended the opening of the Austin, Fort Valley's new Opera House, tonight at 8:30 o'clock. Every seat in the house was taken and many people were turned away. The house seats 750 people besides several boxes accommodating eight or ten persons each. The theatre is owned by George Slappey, one of the most prominent men in Fort Valley, who has made a fortune in this section of the country growing peaches. The building and fixtures complete cost was $15,000. Mr. Slappey is giving the people of this section the very best in modern theatrical attractions and it is expected that the Austin will be liberally patronized."

- *The Leader Tribune, 1919:* "A Fiddlers convention consisting of 40 famous fiddlers will perform at Slappey's Opera House over Braswell's Store. Featured are Fiddling

John Carson, a famous Georgia country musician, and the Lickskillet String Band. Everyone in the community is invited to bring his or her banjo, guitar or other instrument to play along."

Theater Changes Hands Over The Years

The Martin-Thompson theater chain from Hawkinsville leased the theater after Slappey's death in 1934. Slappey was shot and killed on July 20, 1934, by the farm overseer at the Sleepy Hollow Lodge for allegedly making improper advances to the overseer's wife. The overseer was tried in Macon County and found not guilty.

On January 28, 1938, Roy Martin Jr. and E. D. Martin of Muscogee County purchased the building from the Slappey estate for eleven thousand dollars. The Martins tore out the floor of the opera house and installed movie seats on the ground floor where Braswell's store was previously located. The Martins installed a second floor balcony and a third floor projection booth with modern equipment. The new Peach Theater opened on October 24, 1938, with an 800-850 seating capacity.

Its first manager was Harvey H. Whatley of Jonesboro. A later manager during the 1940s was Al Rocke, who

Opening night at Peach Theater in October 1938.

in 1946 started the old Blue Diamond Truck Stop on Highway 41 south of Perry. From 1938 until the late 1940s, the theater experienced its peak years. The Peach Theater closed its doors in early 1970s and was later purchased by Marion Allen, local businessman and former mayor. The theater survived the 1975 tornado without serious damage.

L-R: John Harvard, unidentified person, and Marion Allen in front of Peach Theater in 1955.

Mr. Allen remodeled the old theater to house a discount department store, which later went out of business. In 1999,

Allen donated the property to the Downtown Development Authority (DDA). More recently, Fort Valley's beloved physician, Dr. Dan Nathan, and his son, David Nathan, donated the building on the west side of theater. Both structures provide the DDA with the opportunity to increase tourism in Fort Valley.

Memories of Old Peach Theater

During the forties and fifties, practically everyone converged on the downtown area on Saturdays. The central attraction was the theater. Mr. Al Rocke, theater manager during the forties, stated in a 1974 *Macon Telegraph* article: "On Saturdays, the theater was used by mothers as a child care center. They'd bring the kids in at 10 a.m. on Saturday morning when we opened and the place would be full of kids 'til closing time." Ernest Anderson Jr.: "Saturday was a big day at the movies. You could watch a western, a double feature, a serial and a comedy. Afterwards we would go to Pete and Gus's Candy Kitchen to eat their famous hotdogs." Jimmy Duke: "The admission price was ten cents and for a nickel you could buy a bag of popcorn, a drink or a candy bar." James Khoury: "My friends and I spent all day at the movies on Saturdays. A quarter would cover everything you needed. I bought comic books from the nearby Candy Kitchen." Wilton Walton: "One day I went to visit Billy Sanders. Billy had gone to the show. Mrs. Sanders gave me a dime

Peach County Commission Chairman James Khoury (right) holds a quarter that would cover admission, popcorn, and a drink at the old Peach Theater. Swapping stories of the old theater are L-R: W. L. Brown, William Khoury, Bryant Culpepper, Tom Turner, Wilton Walton, John Dubriel, James Khoury, and Fletcher Barnes.

for admission so I could get in to see Billy." Tom Turner: "Going to the movie in Fort Valley on Saturday was very special. Several times I rode the train from Marshallville for 25 cents plus one cent tax." Calvin Mason: "A hypnotist came there once. He had several people under his control, but couldn't hypnotize me." Beverly Powell: "Several times I borrowed money for theater admission from Dr. Taylor at his drug store and told him to put it on daddy's (Homer Davis) bill."

Future plans for theater restoration

The Fort Valley Downtown Development Authority has owned the old theater building since 1999 when Marion Allen, former Fort Valley mayor (1954-58), donated the building to the City of Fort Valley. With $500,000 approved by the Peach County SPLOST Referendum on July 20, 2004, the Fort Valley DDA has repaired the roof, begun to renovate the interior of the building, and commenced plans to renovate the marquee and façade with an appropriate design and appearance for an early twentieth century building. This project is scheduled to be completed in October 2006.

Upon completion, seating on both the main floor and in the balcony area will be two hundred seats downstairs and fifty seats upstairs. The renovated theater will afford the community an ideal resource to hold plays, recitals, classic movies, concerts, art exhibitions, holiday observances, and business/civic meetings. The restored theater will be called the Austin Theater to revive the original name given it by George Slappey in 1917. The theater restoration project bodes well for the Valley. This innovation is expected to significantly revitalize the downtown area and increase tourism to Fort Valley and Peach County.

Chapter 16
Pete and Gus's Candy Kitchen

Wouvis Brothers Open Candy Kitchen

One of the most popular places in Fort Valley from the 1920s to the mid-1960s was the Candy Kitchen that stood directly beneath the northwest wing of the old Winona Hotel. Its owners were Pete and Gus Wouvis, born in Sparta, Greece. The two brothers came to America in 1904. They settled first in Anderson, South Carolina, and in 1913 came to Fort Valley. By 1920, they had opened the Candy Kitchen on Main Street. Pete died in 1954; Gus passed in 1965 after an extended illness at the Oaks Nursing Home in

Pete and Gus's Candy Kitchen on Main Street circa 1950s.

Marshallville. A cousin from Augusta, Georgia, Joe Bazanos, kept the Candy Kitchen open for about two years while Gus was ill. At Gus's death on January 6, 1965, the establishment closed forever, ending an unforgettable era in Fort Valley's history.

Pete and Gus Hotdogs

The Candy Kitchen's principal drawing card was its delicious hotdogs. The Wouvis brothers brought from Greece a formula for a sauce that would transform an ordinary wiener placed inside a bun to a dish worthy of the gods. The brothers mixed the sauce in the rear of store and kept its ingredients a secret. It was rumored that Jimmy Jordan, an African-American who worked there, knew the ingredients, yet he never revealed the formula. He is now deceased. Pete and Gus's buns were also steamed, which contributed to desirability of the hotdogs. The Wouvises also made and sold candy. At their store on Main Street, you could also buy sodas, chips, ice cream, fruit, nuts, magazines, comic books, and newspapers.

Grady McDaniel, who worked at the Candy Kitchen while Gus was ill, remembers the glory days of the Candy Kitchen. Grady worked there during his sophomore and junior years (1964-65) at Fort Valley High School. Grady worked on Saturdays and during the week after school. He lived on Oak Street behind the Troutman House, a short walking distance from the Candy Kitchen.

His mother, the beloved Grace McDaniel, worked at Armstrong's clothing store, several stores up Main Street from the theater. On Saturday mornings during the 1950s, his mother, on her way to work, would drop off Grady, his brother, Ronnie, and his sister, Frankie, at the Peach Theater. For their supper, she would bring to the theater hotdogs and drinks from Pete and Gus's. Grace's children stayed at the theater until she got off work on Saturday night. Then they walked back home together.

The Secret Sauce

Grady remembers that the hot dog sauce was not of a thick consistency, but was thin and kept warm. Contributing to the taste, he said, were the buns, which were steamed. He especially gave high marks to the peanut brittle candy that was made at the store. Grady said that Jimmy Jordan was the only one remaining who knew the ingredients for the hotdog sauce. "Jimmy carried the formula to his

Grady McDaniel worked at the Candy Kitchen.

grave," remarked Grady. "Anyone with the formula could start a hotdog franchise and become a millionaire."

Many have tried to duplicate the famous hotdog sauce. Ed Dent, who operated a restaurant across from Bobby's Minit Mart

125

during the 1970s, advertised that he had the "Secret Sauce" on a large billboard on Perry highway. Charles Bartlett believes that Mossy Creek Barbeque may be close to perfecting the secret sauce. Julius Shy related that Jack Doles was experimenting with the sauce and had held several hotdog parties for friends.

Dorothy Hudson, president of the Fort Valley Historical Society, has been successful in replicating the formula, according to many townspeople. She experimented with various Greek recipes and produced several versions of the sauce, finally selecting one. Dorothy stated, "The historical society sold hotdogs at Fincher's Park in 1993. We received many complimentary reports from the citizens that the sauce tasted just like Pete and Gus's." Dorothy believes that steaming the buns and boiling the wieners in onion water are also essential.

Dorothy Hudson has attempted to duplicate the Secret Sauce.

Dorothy (my sixth grade teacher at Perry) includes a special ingredient in her "Secret Sauce Recipe" that few cooks would think of, and I am sworn to secrecy. Dorothy isn't about to reveal the recipe for the secret sauce and plans to keep it for future hotdog sales by the historical society.

Pete and Gus Remembered

Joyce Mason: "Pete and Gus lived upstairs in the back of the building. The aroma of the Candy Kitchen–the hotdogs, the sauce, and the onions–was unforgettable. I especially remember the magazine and newspaper racks, and the country and western songbooks you could purchase."

Lewis Moye: "After the movies on Saturday, I went to the Candy Kitchen to eat hotdogs. I especially liked the jellybeans. They used little metal cups to scoop them up. Gus was a volunteer fireman. Two photos of Gus are shown in Fort Valley's Fire Department history published in 1996."

Calvin Mason: "I served with Gus on the volunteer fire department during the 1950s. Gus drove the fire truck and parked it on the street behind the Candy Kitchen. In those days, the Utility

Department, Fire Department, Police Department, and City Hall were all co-located in the alley behind the Candy Kitchen and Winona Hotel."

Bob Marchman: "Gus was a good friend of my mother (former Lois Anderson whose father, Ben Anderson, owned Anderson Drug Store–later became Avera's). Both brothers were members of the Greek Orthodox Church in Macon. Pete never married but Gus married a Macon lady late in life. Mother and Daddy (Robert L. Jr.) carried me to the Candy Kitchen during the 1930s. They would buy me a bun 'without the wiener' covered with Pete and Gus's delicious sauce. It cost five cents. With the wiener, it cost ten cents. When you entered the store, the serving counter was on the left. There were several round tables for customers." Bob described the Wouvis brothers thusly: "Pete was the oldest. He was stocky, medium height, wore glasses, and more reserved than the outgoing Gus. Pete also had more hair than Gus, who was balding." Bob added that Julius Shy recently invited him over for Pete and Gus hotdogs served up by Jack Doles. Bob also revealed that up Main Street from the Candy Kitchen was the old Princess Theater. He said the projection room at the Princess Theater caught fire during the 1930s and that the film operator died in the fire.

Billy Marshall: "During the late 1920s when I was four, my dad, Ben Roe Marshall, took me to the Candy Kitchen. It was Christmastime and I marveled at the candy canes that Pete and Gus had made at their store. As you walked inside the store, the hotdogs were sold in the left-side window area. Seven to eight feet down was the soda fountain. On the right entering the store were the fruit and magazine racks. Gus usually made the hotdogs and Pete worked at the soda fountain. Beyond the counter area were round white tables with chairs. At the back of the store was a room closed to the public. In that room Pete and Gus made the candy and hotdog sauce. Gus was a volunteer fireman. When the fire alarm sounded, he would race out the back door. He drove the smaller fire truck number 2, which had mechanical brakes and was hard to stop. Gus was a mason and got me to join Masonic Lodge 110. My mother, Idel Wooddall, also carried me to the Candy Kitchen. Her father, William Wooddall, was the conductor on the Fort Valley to Atlanta rail line until his death in 1925. In those days the Princess Theater was two doors west of Slappey's Opera House (later became the Peach Theater). The Princess Theater caught on fire during the 1930s. The manager, who came to rescue the projectionist, had to escape through the projection hole in the film operator's room. The projectionist died either from burns or smoke inhalation. After the fire, Christopher's Furniture Company, run by Mr. Paul Janney, moved into the building. Pete and Gus are buried in Oaklawn Cemetery. Both of their middle names are 'John.' A cross stands over each brother's grave. As to replicating Pete and Gus's sauce, Jack Dole's hotdog sauce is 'dead on the money' as far as I can tell."

Wallace Hardeman: "I served with Gus on the volunteer fire department. It was located behind the Candy Kitchen. Gus was usually on call. When the phone rang in the fire department to report a fire, a button in the fire station was punched that set off a bell at the Candy Kitchen. Gus would fly out the back door to crank up the fire truck parked in the alley. I can still see him going out that door with his apron on. He drove truck number 2. Jack Doles seems to have the answer to the Pete and Gus's hotdog sauce."

Tom Turner: "Pete and Gus served up their hotdog sauce with a wooden paddle, then spread finely chopped onions with a spoon. If you purchased four hotdogs, they would place two on a porcelain saucer, then 'criss-cross' the second two on top. They sold fruit—grapes, oranges, apples—on stands in front of store."

Dorothy Hudson: "Bill and I thought a lot of Pete and Gus. They were good to us. When my oldest son, Johnny, was born they came to my house with a present of baby essentials. I visited Jimmy Jordan before his death. Jimmy said, 'I remember you. You are the lady who came in the store every week to buy a *Life* magazine.' I did ask Jimmy if he remembered the recipe for the hotdog sauce, and he replied that he didn't."

Gus Wouvis served in the U.S. Army during World War II. Photo taken in 1942.

Chapter 17
Chris's Liberty Café

City Café in 1927: Between Halprin's and Leader Tribune

Chris Sackellares was born in Thesaly, Greece. He came to the United States in 1912 at the age of sixteen. He married Theodora (Dora) Spahos, also from Greece, in 1923. Chris opened a restaurant in Newnan, Georgia, during the early 1920s. Hearing rumblings of the burgeoning peach industry in Fort Valley and of the success of its 1922-1926 peach festivals that annually drew forty-to-fifty thousand visitors, Chris seized the opportunity and came to Fort Valley in 1927. He opened a restaurant on Main Street called the City Café. It was located across the street from Pete and Gus's Candy Kitchen and sandwiched between Halprin's and the *Leader Tribune*. Halprin's (same building as Express Business Products) was a clothing store owned by Sam Halprin–Muriel Nathan's father. In this location, Chris benefited from the local peach business and the railroad traffic. Muriel Halprin Nathan worked in her father's store as a teenager during the 1930s. She said that tobacco cloth sold for five cents a yard (used to make sheets, bedding, etc), overalls for seventy-nine to ninety-nine cents, and tennis shoes for ninety-eight cents. Muriel met Dan Nathan, a medical student, when she was sixteen and a freshman at the University of Georgia.

Liberty Cafe in 1935

In 1935 Chris moved his restaurant to the south side of Main Street to capture business from travelers coming from the north on Highways 341 and 49 and heading to Florida and points south. He named it the Liberty Café (now the home of Khoury's), after his wife's sister.

Chris Sackellares stands at the front door of the Liberty Café circa 1950s. Photo courtesy: Nick Strickland.

Sackellares Family

Chris and Dora had three children: Helen, Jimmy, and Catherine, the latter two now deceased. Catherine passed at the age of four due to acute appendicitis. Helen

Sackellares graduated from Fort Valley High School with such notables as Christine Davis (Beverly Powell's sister), Jack Hunnicutt, Grover Cleveland, George Hancock, Elaine Morse Clark, and Lillius Harris. At Fort Valley High School, Helen placed first in piano in the district meet in 1943. Helen remarked, "Daddy was so proud of me that he placed a silver dollar under my pillow."

Helen Sackellares Mullis, Chris's daughter and an accomplished pianist.

Helen graduated from Converse College in Spartanburg, South Carolina, with a bachelor's degree in music and a major in piano. She taught Music Education in the public schools and also gave private piano lessons in her home. Helen married King Mullis, a well known Fort Valleyan, now deceased. Helen has one son, Charlie Pappas, who works in the computer field in Atlanta, and three grandsons: Alex and Nick who are twins, age thirteen, and Chase, who is sixteen.

Chris and Dora Sackellares had three grandsons by their son Jimmy and daughter-in-law Evelyn: Chris, a neurologist, engaged in medical research, and Robert and John who are both Georgia Tech engineers.

Inside the Liberty Café

Upon entering the café, you immediately saw the replica of an airplane suspended from the ceiling whose nose propeller blew air throughout the store. "Those were hot days without air conditioning," said Helen. "The airplane fan and the ceiling fans circulated the air." At the back of the store was a large wood-burning stove. A jukebox was stationed near storefront. White tablecloths and napkins adorned the tables. There were stools at the counter for customers who preferred to sit, drink coffee, and just chat with Chris. Coca-Cola calendars were prominent on the walls. Cigarettes and cigars were displayed in a glass showcase at the end of counter. Behind the counter was an old roll-top desk with a typewriter used to type menus.

During the World War II years, complete dinners from soup-to-dessert were thirty-five cents. "During the 1940s, a convoy of soldiers stopped there and completely filled the store," recalled Helen. "We took in a whopping 35 dollars that night, a large sum in those days."

Liberty Cafe, circa 1950. Dora Sackellares behind counter. Photo courtesy: Nick Strickland.

Wouldn't Sell Hotdogs

There was one dish that Chris would not sell and that was a hotdog. The reason he wouldn't is because Pete and Gus Wouvis sold them a few doors down Main Street at their Candy Kitchen. The Sackellareses and Wouvises were close friends and members of the Greek Orthodox Church.

Chris was very generous and kindhearted. He offered free meals to hobos riding on the trains passing through Fort Valley. He poured up free coffee for policemen day or night.

Chris served fresh vegetables daily, preparing them at his restaurant—peas and butter beans were shelled, corn was shucked. He cut his own steaks, ground his hamburger, and sliced his French fries. Milk was delivered daily. Cokes were delivered in cases from the local bottling company. Pies were kept in a safe. "They worked long hours," said Helen. "Mama would open up the store at 6:00 a.m. Daddy would come in around noon and close after midnight.

He often got late business from people getting out of the old Peach Theater and after local ballgames."

Chris cooked with lard. He specialized in omelets and was known for his combination sandwiches. His oyster stew was frequently ordered, but many feel–as I do–that his roast beef sandwiches were his top dish. The "beef gravy" he poured over them was on par with the "secret sauce" used by Pete and Gus on their hotdogs. Helen shared with me the recipe for the beef gravy:

Ingredients: 1-tablespoon real butter, 1-teaspoon sugar, beef stock, and brown coloring.

Directions: Brown the butter and the sugar, adding a little water to dissolve sugar. Then add the mixture to the beef stock left after cooking a beef roast. Add an onion. Boil together the beef stock, onion, and butter-sugar mixture. Add brown coloring (optional) and presto, you have Chris's famous, mouth-watering beef gravy.

Hortman sisters were waitresses during 1950s

Carol Hortman Howell (worked there 1953-1960) and her sister, Minnie Hortman Mathews, (summer of 1954) worked as waitresses at the Liberty Café during the 1950s. Carol said, "During those days, a bottle of coke or cup of coffee cost five cents and a hamburger sold for twenty-five cents." Minnie added, "And you could get a half dozen donuts for twenty-five cents." They both remember the juke box that would play six songs for a quarter. The juke box

Sisters Minnie Mathews and Carol Howell were waitresses at the Liberty Cafe.

featured songs by the Platters, Dean Martin, Doris Day, and Frank Sinatra.

Carol recalled an amusing story about Dora Sackellares. Dora picked up Carol, at the Peach Hotel, located near Woolfolk Chemical Plant, around 5:30 a.m. Then she hurriedly scooted across town to pick up the cook and dishwasher and made it back to the restaurant in time to open by 6:00 a.m. Since it was early morning with virtually no downtown traffic, the police allowed her to run the red light—if no cars were in sight—especially since they got free coffee at Chris' restaurant. One morning a new guy on the force gave Mrs. Sackellares a ticket for running the light. "That made her furious," chuckled Carol. "That killed the policeman's chances of getting any free coffee."

Minnie stated that Chris and the Wouvis brothers were good friends. Chris once told Carol that he had helped Pete and Gus get started in business.

Carol and Minnie provided this interesting list of Fort Valley businessmen who met regularly as a coffee club during the 1950s: John and Lou Armstrong, Layton Shepard Jr., Marion Allen, C.(Cornelius) Hall, Paul Janney, William Khoury Sr., John Houser, Bruce Lee, Albert and Charles Evans, Edrill Tyner Sr., Newt Jordan, Tommy Hunnicutt, Hubbard Stevens, Tom Anthoine, and Spike Reed. They also identified men on the police force during that era: Lynn Chapman, Boisey Barfield, Clyde Pender, R. L. Baggerly, Carl Fergerson, and T. Bellflower.

The Fight that Almost Broke Out

Emory Wilson worked down Main Street at the Candy Kitchen from 1940 to 1944. "Chris visited Pete and Gus at the Candy Kitchen from time to time, and they would sit at a table and speak Greek which no one could understand," stated Emory. Emory said that Pete and Gus represented father figures to him.

During those days, the Candy Kitchen offered curb service. "Cars would line up blowing for service," Emory said. "I would take their order then bring it back on a tray." Emory remembers the famous "secret sauce" for hotdogs being precisely mixed by Pete and Gus with measuring cups. When asked what ingredients the sauce comprised, Emory responded, "I am sure they used vinegar and chili powder. What else, I don't know; however, Robert Wells, who once ran the store while the Wouvises were away, knew the formula."

Emory tells the story of the Fort Valley Green Wave basketball team in 1946—where he was a star player—playing a Marshallville team that featured the tall and talented Johnson brothers. "Marshallville was one of the top teams in Georgia that year," declared Emory. The Green Wave upset Marshallville in a squeaker at the old Marshallville gym in a hotly contested game. After the Friday night game, the Fort Valley team went to the Liberty Café to eat. Soon after they were seated, in came the Marshallville team to eat also. Words were exchanged and chairs started sailing. "Chris had to restore order," chuckled Emory.

End of an Era

During the early 1960s, Chris retired and closed the Liberty Café forever. Chris and Dora continued to live in Fort Valley. Chris went to be with the Lord in 1976. His funeral was held at the Fort Valley United Methodist Church with its pastor, Rev. Carlton Anderson, officiating. Soon thereafter, his wife, Dora, joined the Methodist Church. She passed in 1990. Both are buried in Oaklawn Cemetery. Chris and Dora were two of Fort Valley's finest citizens, loved and respected by everyone.

Chapter 18
Newsprint and Bookshelves: History of Peach County Newspapers and Libraries

*Danny and Julie Evans proudly display the **Leader Tribune,** the legal organ of Peach County.*

1859 newspaper found at the *Leader Tribune*

The November 1, 1859, edition of the *Nineteenth Century* newspaper was found among the *Leader Tribune's* archives. This was Fort Valley's earliest known newspaper (circa 1857-1866) and was published in downtown Fort Valley in an upstairs office opposite the carriage factory. Editor was F. Lafayette Cherry and John A. Burton its publisher. A subscription charge was two dollars a year. Advertisements sold for one dollar per square inch for first insertion and fifty cents thereafter.

It contains five items of interest: (1) Newspaper published an advertisement to sell its old hand press. It planned to buy a new power press to cope with an increase in subscriptions. (2) A graphic account of the hanging of murderer James Revell at Knoxville, Georgia, in Crawford County on October 21, 1859. Attending the hanging were three thousand curiosity seekers. (3) A visit by editor Cherry to the Fort Valley Female Seminary (chartered 1852) at the corner of College and Miller Streets. The editor noted that seventy students were attending the academy and heaped praise on teachers Professor G. H. Holcomb, Mrs. M. E. Starke, and Miss Julia Brown. A local physician, Dr. W. J. Simpson, lectured there every Wednesday afternoon. (4) Although abhorrent, the paper reads: "Sales of Negroes must be made at public auction on the first Tuesday of the month." This was the pre-Civil War era. (5) Local advertisers were W. J. Anderson's Clothing Store, W. A. Wiggins Drug Store, A. H. Long's Book Store, W. L. Sloan's Watch and Jewelry Store, Dunlap and Harris Grocery Store, Miss Smith's Millinery Shop, and Dr. David N. Austin's hospital.

Dr. Austin (1817-1879) operated on Confederate troops at an old schoolhouse during the Civil War. Dr. Austin, who married Emily M. Braswell, was the father of Mariah and Samuel "Bully" Austin. Mariah married Will Kersh, co-editor of the *Fort Valley Enterprise* (published in 1880s). Bully was a good friend of George W. Slappey. Slappey named his opera house the Austin Theater after Bully Austin. Slappey was killed by the farm overseer at the Sleepy Hollow Lodge in 1934 for allegedly making advances toward the overseer's wife. After the sensational murder, Slappey's lodge became haunted.

Newspaper history: 1860s-1890s

- *Fort Valley Ledger* appeared in 1866. The publisher was Dennis W. Booley. It was sold to J. W. Love and renamed the *Fort Valley Gazette.*
- *Southwest Georgian* edited by Joel R. Griffin. It was published in Macon and circulated in Fort Valley from 1870-71.
- *Fort Valley Mirror* was first published in 1872 by W.T. Christopher.
- *Fort Valley Enterprise* was in publication during 1888, the same year that the Atlanta and Florida Railroad was completed to Fort Valley. Will Kersh and Will Wynne were co-owners and co-editors.
- *Fort Valley Leader* emerged during the 1890s—the merger of two newspapers: the *Leader* and the *Enterprise.* Thomas Virgil Fagan (great uncle of Marcus Hickson) was proprietor and Bully Austin, editor.

*The **Leader Tribune** was located on the north side of Main Street. Photo circa 1930.*

Leader Tribune history: 1888-present

- The *Leader Tribune* was established in 1888; however, only sketchy information is available prior to 1920. That's because the 1969 fire at the Thomas Public Library destroyed valuable newspaper archives.
- Thomas J. Shephard purchased the *Leader Tribune* in 1898 (*History of Peach County Georgia,* page 409). Peach County history mentions three other editors: Dan Bickers, Walter R. Branham, and Mark M. Mathews. Their tenures are estimated to have occurred between the early 1900s and 1917.
- Available newspaper archives reveal Thomas N. Jarrell as editor in 1917 and Joel Martin Mann as editor during 1920-24.
- John H. Jones was owner and editor: 1925-1952. Office located on Main Street.
- Dan Grahl was owner and editor: 1952-1974. Grahl purchased the *Leader Tribune* from John H. Jones in 1952 and published his first edition on August 7, 1952. In 1961 Grahl moved the office from Main Street to Vineville Street

where Wilder's Garage sits today. Mr. Grahl, who served in the Georgia House of Representatives from 1964 to 1974, died in November 1974. Mrs. Mildred Grahl sold the paper to Wilton Walton on February 1, 1975.

- Wilton Walton, owner and editor: 1975-1984. His office was on West Main Street next to Evans Park. Walton sold the newspaper to Bob Tribble of Manchester on February 1, 1984.
- Tribble Publications: 1984 to present. Office is located at 109 Anderson Avenue. Tribble owns a newspaper chain comprising 31 newspapers. Previous editors were Cindy and Chuck Morley (now at *Fayette Daily News*), Hallie Rigdon, Mike Lovvorn, and Vicky Davis.

Leader Tribune staff in 2004: Front, L-R: Sheryl Collins, Judy Robinson, Editor Vicky Davis, Cally Whitehead. Back row: A. W. Dorsey, Victor Kulkosky, Michael Phillips, Lee Posey.

- In November 2005, Danny Evans, a highly respected and successful newspaperman and owner of Evans Newspapers Inc., a newspaper conglomerate, became co-owner with Tribble Publications of the *Leader Tribune*. Evans serves as both publisher and editor. His wife, Julie, is advertising director. Other full time staff members are: Stacey Shy, office manager; Lula Alice Batchelor, bookkeeping; Nathan Mathis, advertising; Victor Kulkosky, news reporter; and Faye Jones, a popular and renowned writer, who also covers the Byron news.

Thomas J. Shepard: editor 1898 to circa 1910

When the Methodist Church was built in 1901, Shepard placed a copy of the newspaper in the church cornerstone. He was Fred Shepard's uncle and affectionately known as "Uncle Tom Shepard." He taught the boys Sunday School class at the Methodist Church for many years. According to David Sammons, when the cornerstone was removed in 1990 during the church's sesquicentennial, the newspaper was found stored in a metal box and badly deteriorated.

John H. Jones: editor 1925-1952

John H. Jones was publisher-editor, Alvah Culpepper was associate editor, and Jones' wife, Margaret, was editor and general manager. Billy Marshall has a 1931 photo of his 3rd grade class which shows Jones' daughter, Peggy, as his classmate. Billy said that the Jones family lived in the house that is now Rook's funeral home. Jones later became postmaster according to Fred Shepard.

Dan Grahl: 1952-1974

Judge Bryant Culpepper, who reported on Fort Valley Green Wave football during the early 1960s, remembers Grahl: "Mr. Grahl was a fine man, a gentleman and a scholar. He had a deep musical voice and could often be seen at the Main Street office working on the old linotype machine preparing the newspaper for printing. During hot days he would sit near the front with the doors open. He worked with his sleeves rolled up and wore a green visor. He loved his Lord, was a student of the Bible, and taught the Adult Bible Class at the Methodist Church. He combined work with politics and effectively served in the Georgia General Assembly for ten years. As a politician and newspaper man, Mr. Grahl was the spoken and written conscience of the Fort Valley community. He loved the Lord and he loved Fort Valley."

Wilton Walton: 1975-1984

Vicky Davis stated that Walton "ran a first class newspaper." His newspaper office was located on West Main Street next to Evans Park. His wife, the former Ann Facey of Bedford England, was an integral part of the newspaper operation.

Vicky Davis: 1997-2005

Vicky Davis, a seasoned veteran with over thirty years experience in newspaper work, had previously served as editor of four newspapers: *Hawkinsville Dispatch, Richmond Hill-Bryan County News, Claxton Enterprise*, and *Robins Review*.

The *Peach County Enterprise:* 1970-75

The *Peach County Enterprise* burst on the scene in 1970, but went out of business after five years. Its first publisher was J. Frank Hague III and first editor was Jimmy Bennett. Mr. Ruben of Cordele purchased the paper around 1973. Bob Gilreath became editor and Twila Gresham associate editor.

Byron Newspapers

Billy Tucker and David Von Almen started the *Byron Gazette* in 1989. In 1990, Tucker partnered with his sister, Ann Tunali. The first editor was Andy McGill. He was succeeded by Cornelia "Pete" Nichols in 1994. Nichols, who earlier served five years with the *Leader Tribune,* retired in 2001. The *Gazette* staff comprised Faye Jones, feature editor and Marie Ross, office manager. Bryon historian Jackie Edwards was a longtime contributor. The Gazette was sold to the CNHI news group in 1997. Knight-Ritter bought the *Byron Gazette* in 2001. It was discontinued and converted to a tabloid shopper.

Historians Betsy Murdock and Frances McDaniel remember the *Byron News* being published during the 1960s. The owner, editor, and location are unknown.

Technological Advances in Newspaper Production

The first method of printing involved the hand-setting of every print character. Introduction of the "linotype machine" provided newspapers with the capability to produce an entire line of type from print characters exposed to molten lead. With the advent of electronic typewriters, newspapers began pasting newspaper script and photos on the page to be printed. Now human hands never touch the newspaper. Script and photo layout are accomplished on a computer screen. The newspaper is transmitted for printing electronically.

History of Peach County Public Libraries

Fort Valley had library as early as 1878

A. C. Riley Sr. (Fort Valley mayor: 1888-90) wrote in the local newspaper, dated August 12, 1880, that a library existed in Fort Valley during 1878, which "attractively housed 2500 volumes of choice and well-selected reading matter, eight first-class daily papers, numerous weeklies, and several standard magazines." Its name, location, and librarian are unknown.

Thomas Public Library Organized: 1915

During the early 1900s, Dr. Edward Gray Thomas, a native of Butler and an Atlanta dentist, moved to Fort Valley and built a house at 312 College Street, the present home of Thomas and Cynthia Yount. Dr. Thomas practiced dentistry in what is now the Yount's living room. His wife, the former Lula Tyner, was a book lover who had amassed quite a collection of books. Mrs. Thomas assisted in her husband's dental practice and, from the reception desk, loaned books from the Thomas' personal library to patients and local citizens.

With interest growing toward establishing a public library, a meeting of thirty-seven community leaders was held in the Thomas' home on September 15, 1915. From this meeting the Fort Valley Library Association was formed and the decision made to open a library. To provide an initial repository of books, Mrs. Thomas donated her collection of five hundred books. She also encouraged others to donate books and equipment. Eight days later on September 23, 1915, the library opened its doors in a rent-free room on the second floor of the Evans Building on Main Street. Seventeen citizens pledged one dollar a month to pay the librarian's salary.

In 1916, in recognition of the contributions of Dr. and Mrs. Thomas, the library association was renamed the Thomas Library Association. In 1917, the Presbyterian pastor, Rev. Irons, a strong and persistent supporter, succeeded in getting the Fort Valley City government to commit twenty-five dollars a month to fund the library.

When Dr. and Mrs. Thomas both died in 1930, part of their estate (twenty thousand dollars in 1930 dollars) was left to the library as a trust fund called the Lula Thomas Endowment Fund.

A nephew of Dr. Thomas tried to break the will, but the Chairman of Board of Trustees, David C. Strother, successfully fought the suit.

During the early 1920s, the library association was replaced with a board of trustees. Its first chairman was Ralph Newton (first County School Superintendent) who served until 1929. David C. Strother was chairman thirty-four years, from 1929 to 1963. Barnett Bleckley was chairman from 1963 to 1966. He was succeeded by Felton Hatcher who served until after the new library was built on the corner of Persons and Miller Streets. Others who served as trustee chairpersons since Hatcher are Sam Culpepper, Ann Blair Brown, and Sue Gillis Leslie, the current chairperson.

On July 23, 1971, an agreement was signed by Fort Valley Mayor Paul Reehling, J. D. Doles, County Commission Chairman, and Felton Hatcher, trustee chairman, regarding the appointment of library trustees and designating the Thomas Public Library as headquarters for the Peach County Public Library System with Byron serving as its branch.

Thomas Public Library in 2004

Succession of Librarians/Directors

(1) Miss Parmelee Cheves: 1915 to 1924, (2) Miss Gena Riley (Fort Valley mayors A. C. Riley Sr. and A. C. Riley Jr. were her father and brother): 1924-1956, (3) Mrs. Gertrude Jones: 1956-1973, (4) Mrs. Ann Dalton: 1973-1974, (5) Jimmy Smith: 1974-1988, (6) Mrs. Gilda Stanbery-Cotney: 1988-present.

Thomas Public Library Staff in 2004. Front, L-R: Director Gilda Stanberry-Cotney, Coretta Prater McKenzie, Jane Matthews, Nancy Rairdon. Back, L-R: Karin C. Martin-Lopez, Billy Tripp, Frances Bowden, and Ron White, Byron branch manager.

Locations of Thomas Public Library

(1) Evans Building, located on the corner of Main Street and Camellia Blvd: 1915 to 1936. By the mid-1930s, space in the Evans Building was inadequate. In planning the Peach County courthouse built in 1936, Judge Millard C. Moseley, ordinary and county manager, proposed constructing an annex to be used as a library. Separated by a firewall, the library had a separate entrance on Central Avenue.

(2) Peach County Courthouse annex facing Central Avenue: 1936-1969. From 1936 to 1969, the book volume grew from seven thousand to twenty-four thousand books. On December 5, 1969, a fire gutted the library and burned fifteen thousand books with the remainder damaged by water. The *Leader Tribune*, December 11, 1969, reported that arson was suspected. Mollie Jones Culpepper of Perry, whose mother, Mrs. Gertrude Jones, was librarian, remembers her mother working long and hard hours to salvage wet and smoke-damaged books. She said the library was moved into the Steed family home across Central Avenue—now the Grace House. Helping reopen the library at this new location were Mrs. C. A. Vinson, assistant librarian, and Mrs. Connie Flowers.

(3) Vacant residence on Central Avenue: 1969-1972.

(4) New 5,600 sq. ft. library constructed on corner of Persons and Miller Streets: 1972-1998; expanded to 10,100 sq. ft. in 1984.

(5) By the mid-1990s, the library on Persons and Miller Streets had fallen below minimum space standards. Due to growing book volume and inadequate space to convert the archaic card catalog system to an automated program for cataloguing and resource sharing with fifty-six library systems in Georgia, a new 17,502 sq. ft. library was opened on Martin Luther King Jr. Drive in 1998, the first Superfund/Brownfields development project in Georgia.

In 1961, a branch library was opened on State University Drive in a building adjacent to the Gano Building. This brought the resources of the public library to the black communities in the Gano and Tabor Heights Project areas. Mrs. Evelyn McCray, its first librarian, speaks in glowing terms of the reading enrichment and help on school projects the library afforded the children of that era. This branch closed in 1985.

Byron Library

Although Byron had a small library as early as 1930 beside Dr. James B. Kay's office, the Byron Public Library, with four hundred books donated by the Thomas Public Library, opened in

1936 as a Works Progress Administration (WPA) project under President Roosevelt's New Deal. At termination of the WPA, the Byron library was operated under the direction of the Thomas Public Library. The library served as a public and school library for many years. Mrs. Lena Adair Kay (Dr. Kay's wife and Lena Belle Duke's mother) and the Byron Woman's Club were very instrumental in promoting the library.

Successive locations of the Byron library were: (1) Wooden Building (former post office and telephone exchange) next to Dr. Kay's office: 1930-1936, (2) Dupree's Store (Main Street): 1936-1939, (3) Byron Public School: 1939-1944, (4) Old City Jail: 1944-1956, (5) Downtown Store: 1956-1975, (6) Byron City Complex: 1975-1985, (7) New 4,255 sq. ft. library built on Church Street: 1985-present; expanded to 6255 sq. ft. in 1997.

Byron librarians over the years were: (1) Mrs. Mattie Dupree: 1930-1936, (2) Mrs. Iona Dupree: 1936-1939, (3) Mrs. Susie Allen: 1939-1942, (4) Mrs. Ella Pender: 1942-1944, (5) Mrs. H.M. Davis: 1944-1946, (6) Mrs. Susie McNiece: 1946-1969, (7) Mrs. Sara B. Batchelor: 1969-1980, (8) Mrs. Catherine Smith: 1980-2000, (9) Miss Ashley Moore: 2000-2002, (10) Jeff Ervin: 2002-2003, (11) Ron White: Oct 2003-2005, (12) Susan Halbedel: 2005-present.

Peach County Library System today

The Peach County Library System maintains forty-three computers (acquired and replaced solely with grant monies), fourteen for staff and twenty-nine for use by library patrons. Patrons use the internet to access information on books, electronic journals, magazines, and encyclopedias; send electronic mail; apply for jobs, scholarships, and take courses on-line; perform historical and genealogical research; participate in on-line book clubs; view community calendars and events; and keep abreast of state, national, and world news.

The summer reading program has achieved great success. Expanded beyond the traditional reading for fun and enlightenment, it now includes story-telling and guest appearances by artists and authors to inspire young people and to engender learning.

The combined staffs of Fort Valley and Byron number eight fulltime and four part-time personnel. This professional and service-oriented staff maintains 57,130 titled books, serves 8400 registered patrons, and accommodates over fifty-eight thousand visitors annually. Georgia Governor Zell Miller recognized the library for being in the top 10 percent in the state based on services provided. Approximately 60 percent of library funding is provided by the county, the remainder by state appropriations and various grants.

At the helm of operations is Mrs. Gilda Stanbery-Cotney, a proactive and progressive director, who has served with distinction for eighteen years, providing outstanding library services to Peach County.

Chapter 19
Walking Tall:
History of Peach County Sheriff's Department

Succession of Peach County Sheriffs:

George D. Anderson Sr.: Jan 20, 1925 to Nov 11, 1930
George Anderson was the first sheriff after creation of Peach County in November 1924. He lived at Myrtle, a settlement between Fort Valley and Perry where he was a peach farmer and owned a packing shed. Anderson died in office during November 1930. The *Leader Tribune*, dated Nov 13, 1930, reported his funeral at the Methodist Church. His wife, the former Clara Phillips, had died three years earlier. Their children were: Mrs. Robert Harris, Mrs. Doddridge Houser, Miss Juliette Anderson, Hugh Anderson, and George D. Anderson Jr. Sheriff Anderson was the grandfather of Claire Houser Dodd, Mary Killen Houser Hammond, George Ann Harris Seymour, Robert Ligon Harris, and Henry E. Harris.

Elbert Briggs Fagan: December 30, 1930 to March 6, 1936
Fagan served five years as chief deputy under Sheriff Anderson. On December 5, 1930, Fagan won the election without opposition to fill the unexpired term of Sheriff Anderson. In the 1932 election, Fagan won over Robert J. Taylor. In the February 27, 1936 election, Fagan beat C. P. Barrett 679 votes to 472. Fagan died on March 6, 1936, of influenza, a week after the election. Briggs Fagan's funeral was held at the Presbyterian Church, officiated by Rev. William C. Sistar, and assisted by Methodist pastor, Rev J. H. Houser. He was survived by his mother, Mrs. Julian Fagan, one daughter Elizabeth, age nine, and Claude Fagan of Perry. Fagan's wife, the former Miss Omie Terry, had died earlier in February 1935. Fagan was a cousin of Marcus Hickson Jr., whose mother was a Fagan.

Edward Glen Fagan: March 12, 1936 to April 2, 1936
On March 12, 1936, Judge and County Ordinary M.C. Moseley of Byron appointed Edward Glen Fagan, a cousin of Briggs Fagan, to serve until a special election could be held on April 2, 1936. Glen Fagan was the uncle of Marcus Hickson Jr., whose mother was Louise Fagan.

John Emsley Lee: April 2, 1936 to May 15, 1943

John Lee won the April 2, 1936 election over Glen Fagan 507 votes to 346. Sheriff Lee hired no deputies. After serving seven years, Lee resigned to take a position with the Federal Internal Revenue Service. Lee was the grandfather of John, Ann, and Jerry Lee.

Police Chief Grady Cochran: May 15, 1943 to June 23, 1943

Fort Valley Police Chief Cochran was appointed sheriff on May 15, 1943, to serve until a special election. Boisey Barfield was named interim police chief. In the June 11, 1943, election, Cochran lost to Herbert Beeland, and returned to his former position of police chief where he served until his retirement in 1970. Cochran is the father of Virginia Cochran Howard.

Herbert Beeland: June 23, 1943 to December 31, 1964

Herbert Beeland was elected on June 11, 1943, to fill the vacancy of Sheriff John Lee. Beeland retired from office after serving twenty-two years. He is the grandfather of Matt, Jimbo, Reggie, and Holly Mullis.

J. Reginald Mullis: January 1, 1965 to December 31, 1980

Reg Mullis, who married Beeland's daughter, Joyce, and served as Beeland's deputy for over three years, defeated three opponents—Garnett Pirkle, Frank Flowers, and Sol Vining Jr.—in the March 12, 1964, election. He is the father of Matt, Jimbo, Reggie, and Holly Mullis.

Johnnie V. Becham: January 1, 1981 to December 31, 2004

Prior to running for sheriff, Johnnie Becham served approximately seven years with the Fort Valley Police Department (1961-1968) and approximately eleven years with the Sheriff's Department (1968-1980). Becham defeated Reg Mullis in the 1980 primary election and successfully defended his office against opposition in 1988, 1996, and 2001. After twenty-four years as sheriff, Becham retired on December 31, 2004. His wife is the former Lucy Ray. Their son, Kim, is also employed by the sheriff's department.

Terry W. Deese: January 1, 2005-present

Terry Deese won the July 25, 2004 primary election over challenger Ricky Vining and took office on January 1, 2005. His wife is the former Karen Johnson. Their children are Kelly and Michael.

Shot at, wounded, run over, and left for dead

Johnnie Becham cannot match the size and brawn of the legendary Tennessee Sheriff Buford Pusser portrayed in the block-buster movie *Walking Tall,* but Johnnie's career has been equally sensational. Johnnie has been shot at, wounded, run over, and left for dead.

On August 14, 1985, Johnnie received a call that marijuana was being sold near Mose Appling's Garage on State University Drive. To conceal his identity, Johnnie removed his badge and uniform and drove to the site in plain clothes. When he arrived, he noticed a truck parked near the garage. Upon inspecting the truck, he found inside the truck a bag containing plastic packets of marijuana and a pistol. Before Johnnie could remove the marijuana bag, the truck's owner walked up, jumped in the truck and proceeded to drive off. "I was leaning into the truck trying to grab the ignition key as he drove off," stated Johnnie. "He carried me about two hundred feet down the road before shoving me out." Johnnie spun and hit the pavement on his back, the truck's rear wheels running over his right arm and leg. An ambulance was dispatched to the scene to transport Johnnie to the Peach County hospital. Miraculously, he survived.

As reported in the September 10, 1986, issue of the *Leader Tribune,* Sheriff Becham, Sgt. Donnie Martin, Chief Deputy Jimmy Jones, Sgt. Terry Deese, and Deputy Kenny Cameron went to a house on Chapman Road near Byron about 3:00 p.m. on September 5, 1986, to serve a search warrant. An earlier stakeout had revealed that marijuana was being grown there. The search of the premises found marijuana seeds inside the house and marijuana plants growing in the woods behind the house. After gathering the evidence and completing the search, the five officers departed. Chief Deputy Jones and Deputy Cameron had departed the driveway in separate cars and turned onto Chapman Road. The third car with Sgt. Martin driving and Sgt. Deese as passenger was proceeding down the driveway with Sheriff Becham the last to leave. Suddenly a man started firing a 30-06 rifle from the yard. The first shots hit Sheriff Becham's car, bullet fragments striking him in the shoulder. The second series hit Sgt. Martin's car, also wounding him in the shoulder. Sgt. Martin crawled out of the car into a ditch with Sgt. Deese trying to cover him. Deputy Cameron doubled back and began returning fire. Shooting from the house ceased. Chief Deputy Jones drove Sheriff Becham and Sgt. Martin to the hospital. Middle Georgia law enforcement agencies were called to the scene. The shooter did not surrender until 3: 18 a.m. the next morning—another harrowing experience for Sheriff Becham who could have been killed along with Sgt. Martin and Sgt. Deese. Lucy Becham vividly remembers receiving notification when Johnny was shot and when he was run over. On both occasions she didn't know how badly he was hurt until she arrived at the hospital. For Lucy's enduring support and for always being there for him, Johnnie gave her a dozen red roses.

Sheriff Johnnie Becham (R) investigates a murder scene on the Norfolk Southern railroad in Fort Valley. In the background is railroad overpass bridge. At left is Calvin Mason, long time Fort Valley businessman and local historian.

Old County Jail Closed and New Jail Built

Old Jail built in 1927

At the request of Judge Cloud Morgan, the County Commissioners closed the old jail—built in 1927—for security reasons in July 1984. In 1985, a one percent sales tax was passed to build a new 23,000 square-foot jail costing $ 2,980,086. Also, fifty acres of land was acquired for $ 64,000. The current jail, completed in December 1988, has thirty-two cells with an eighty-bed capacity. The average occupancy is sixty-four to sixty-eight prisoners. The sheriff's department employs fifty-eight personnel. Recent passage of the one percent SPLOST in July 2004 includes building another jail pod comprising twelve

New Jail built in 1988

cells.

Since Peach County was created in 1924, its citizens have been blessed with outstanding sheriffs. Current Sheriff Terry Deese continues the outstanding tradition of his predecessors.

Chapter 20
The Scooter: Fort Valley Football Legend, Wesley (Scooter) Melvin

The Scooter's defining moment:

"No one can catch Scooter Melvin on the football field." This was the assessment of Fort Valley's Hall of Fame coach Norman Faircloth. Entertaining a vastly different opinion were the Hawkinsville Red Devils led by legendary football coach Bobby Gentry. That's because Hawkinsville boasted of Melvin Borum, one of the fastest speedsters in the entire state, if not the fastest.

If Wesley Melvin breaks through our defensive secondary, Melvin Borum will surely run him down, the Red Devils thought. Since the Fort Valley Green Wave and the Red Devils had fought to a zero to zero tie earlier in the 1952 season, a playoff game was held in Cordele, a neutral site, to crown the region champion.

Coach Faircloth anticipated that Hawkinsville, on opening kickoff, would not kick the ball in Wesley's direction, so he devised a plan to exploit Hawkinsville's strategy.

As expected, Hawkinsville's kickoff sailed straight to Gresham Aultman on the opposite side of field. Aultman fielded the ball at the ten yard line and headed toward a wall of blockers on his left. At the last second, he handed the ball off to Melvin on a reverse. Wesley side-stepped several would-be tacklers and headed down the sideline.

Hawkinsville's safety Melvin Borum anticipated the reverse and quickly fell in behind Wesley in hot pursuit. At the thirty-yard line, Borum was less than five yards behind. At mid-field, Wesley could feel Borum breathing down his neck.

A lot of things probably went through Wesley's mind. Was he going to disappoint his coach who said no one could catch him? Was he ready to suffer the heckling of Red Devil fans who would gloat if Borum tackled him?

Wesley could traverse a hundred yards in a track meet in 10.2 seconds, but with a football cradled under his arm and the Green Wave faithful cheering, his feet took on magical wings that glided him effortlessly across the gridiron. With Borum closing fast, and the pride of the Green Wave on the line, the Scooter reached deep down inside himself and turned on the after burners.

A foot race to the goal line ensued: Forty...thirty...twenty... ten...Touchdown! Ninety yards for the score and the game was only seconds old! Fort Valley's fans erupted in jubilation. Hawkinsville was stunned and silent.

Wesley Melvin turns on the after burners on his famous touchdown run against Hawkinsville.

The play as recounted by Coach Norman Faircloth

Listen now to the immortal words of Coach Faircloth, who described the touchdown run: "Our little team ran on the field and began warming up. Hawkinsville ran onto the field looking like the University of Alabama. They had so many talented players and were so big. The Hawkinsville fans all stood up and started taunting and yelling 'Bye, bye, Scooter.' Well, on the opening kickoff, we pulled a reverse with Gresham handing the ball to Wesley. The Hawkinsville fans were right. It was bye, bye, Scooter. He went ninety yards for the touchdown on the opening kickoff. We downed Hawkinsville 20 to 12 for the region championship."

The Goal Line Stalker

Wesley Melvin lettered in football in 1950-1953. Used purely as a defensive player his freshman year, Wesley scored 89 points as a sophomore, 102 as a junior, and 112 as a senior for a total of 303 points in three years as a tailback—the equivalent of fifty touchdowns. Wesley also lettered in track all four years, running the 100-yard-dash, 220-yard-dash, and 880-yard-relay. Fort Valley captured the district track meet nine years in a row (1946-1954), its chief opponent being Perry. "We always had to fight it out with Perry to win district," remarked Wesley. One of Wesley's proudest accomplishments is making a perfect score of 100 on the State Spelling Contest. Confirmation of this feat is a certificate from the Georgia High School Association, dated April 7, 1954, and signed by Executive Secretary Sam Burke.

During Wesley's four years at Fort Valley High School, the Green Wave team won thirty-eight games against only six losses and one tie. During this span the Green Wave won two region titles (1950 and 1952) and two state runner-up crowns the same two years. The 1950 team went eleven wins against only one loss; the 1951 team won nine and lost one; in 1952, the record was ten wins, two losses and one tie; and during Wesley's senior year, the 1953 team won eight and lost two.

In 1954, Wesley was named the "Middle Georgia Player of the Year" by the *Macon Telegraph and News*, "Back of the Year" by the *Atlanta Journal and Constitution* and named to the "All Southern" team. Wesley was also named to the "All-State" team his junior and senior years. In 1953, he was honored by the Macon Touchdown Club as "Player of the Week." He was also honored by the Fort Valley Lion's Club in 1954.

Superintendent Ernest Anderson presents "Middle Georgia Player of the Year" trophy to Wesley Melvin in 1954 as Coach Norman Faircloth looks on.

Identifiable team members: 1950-53 FVHS football teams

Nick Strickland, Gresham Aultman, Ernest (Moose) Murray, Eddie Merritt, Richard Aultman, Jack Newberry, Wilton Walton, Strib McCants, Pat Swan, Tommy Fagan, James Bozeman, Henry Wheaton, Bobby Holly, Wilder Dent, Bobby Mason, Tommy Branan, Billy Bankston, Butch Anthoine, Jimmy Pearson, Delmar Fennell, Charles Barfield, Ted Joyner, Buddy Wilson, Johnny Bellflower, Charles Scarbrough, Ralph Bassett, Joe Clarke, Sinclair Frederick,

Cecil Martin, Donnie Weinberger, Royce Collins, Bill Schofill, Gene Crowe, Feddie Barnes, Oliver Snapp, Joel Hobbs, Phil Mathews, Jimmy Rasnake, Dickey Watkins and Jimmy Stephens.

Commentaries on the Scooter

Gresham Aultman, *Leader Tribune,* July 31, 1975, reprinted a 1954 quote: "Wesley is the hardest man to tackle I have ever seen. It was an experience in itself playing with him. He was a great guy."
Coach Faircloth, *Leader Tribune,* July 31, 1975, reprinted a 1954 quote: "Melvin's sense of balance was uncanny. I have seen him hit so low and so hard, that he turned a complete flip in the air, came down on his feet, and continued running with the football." Also in the *Macon Telegraph,* January 14, 1954, Coach Faircloth, stated, "Wesley Melvin is the greatest competitor, pound for pound, that I have ever coached." Wesley was 5 feet, 6 inches and weighed 145 pounds.
Bob Oliver, *Macon Telegraph* Sports Writer, December 19, 1953, wrote: "Few took advantage of strong blocking as did the Scooter. He also had the power, despite his size to make holes for himself, and he had no peer at returning punts and kickoffs. He was a terror in the open field...He was personification on the gridiron and it will be a long interim before the likes of him will again come down the Middle Georgia football pike."
Dan Grahl, editor of the *Leader Tribune*, 1953, wrote: "Wesley was a marked man through out the ball game. Hawkinsville had several players whose only job was to cover Melvin. He was tackled viciously and frequently by three or four men at a time. He always walked away under his own power and threw himself into the next play just that much harder. His sprint for the touchdown was a beauty to behold."
Wilton Walton, teammate: "I was in the class behind Wesley Melvin and had a view of Wesley that not many others had ... of his cleats as he ran over me time after time in practice. Lucky I didn't have to face him in real combat. Of course, we also got to sit in the locker room at halftime and to hear Coach Faircloth breathe fire and brimstone as he raised the emotional level of his players. Wesley worked as hard at practice as he did in a game. He never had a bad day. It was always full speed. Wesley made the team on defense in the 9th grade. He was one of the best downfield tacklers I've ever seen. He was afraid of no one, no matter the size. Combine that with his speed and Wesley became awesome. Coach Faircloth

often said that Wesley might not be the fastest person in the world, but he was the fastest he had seen in a full uniform."

Coach Bobby Gentry, Hawkinsville's Hall of Fame football coach (1948-1976): "Wesley Melvin was a real competitor. Not only was he a good football player, he was a good person. When you played Fort Valley, you had better make plans to stop Wesley because he could go all the way on any snap. In 1952, we had tied Fort Valley in the regular season and had to play them on Thanksgivings day in Cordele for the region championship. Wesley ran the opening kick-off back for a touchdown. He was a 145 pound back who ran like a 190 pounder. Without question, he could play this day in time. Our players had great respect for Wesley."

Wesley Melvin, *Macon Telegraph,* December 19, 1953: "The best team we played against was the 1953 Hawkinsville team and the best player I ever faced was Melvin Borum of Hawkinsville." July 1, 2004: "Hawkinsville coach Bobby Gentry was one of Georgia's greatest football coaches and a fine gentleman."

A half century later

Following graduation Wesley played football at Austin-Peay University, but after a career-ending injury, he returned to Fort Valley. He met his wife, Kay Hinger of Latrobe, Pennsylvania, on a blind date while in the army. They have been married for forty-six years and reside in Fort Valley. This union produced two daughters: Kasey, the oldest, a child psychologist in New Bern, North Carolina, and Barbara, who lives in

L-R: Wesley Melvin, cheerleader Elizabeth (Libba) Shepard, and majorettes Sue Lester and Betty Jordan.

Charleston, South Carolina, and serves as governmental liaison for the South Carolina Ports Authority. Wesley and Kay are now retired, Wesley from Blue Bird and Royster Clark Inc. and Kay from the Citizens Bank.

The old high school on Knoxville Street is a relic of its storied past, Anderson Field has moved, and bouncing balls are no longer heard from the old gym, yet to this day the memories of Wesley Melvin and all the football and basketball players of that era remain alive in the hearts and minds of those who proudly call themselves the "Fort Valley Green Wave."

Chapter 21
State Championship teams from the Valley

Fort Valley High School:
1952 State Championship Basketball Team (undefeated)

First row, left to right: Dickie Watkins, Daniel Fennell, Jimmy Thomson, Strib McCants, Eddie Merritt, Richard Aultman.
Second row: Coach Norman Faircloth, Ted Joyner, Pat Swan, Ed Beck, Oliver Snapp, Vernon Bowden.

Fort Valley High School:
1954 State Championship Basketball Team (undefeated)

Front row, L-R: Butch Anthoine, Billy Clark, Tommy Fagan. Second row: Henry Wheaton, Ronnie Teece, Tommy Branan, Joe Clarke. Third row: Delmar Fennell, Gresham Aultman, Ed Beck, Eddie Merritt, Buddy Wilson.

Fort Valley High School:
1961 State Championship Basketball Team

Front, L-R: Tee Faircloth, Dave Hardeman, Richard Lawhorne, Ronnie McDaniel, Dan Harrelson, Jody Hardeman. Back row: Manager Charles Bailey, Ronnie Hortman, Ray Pearson, David Nathan, Herbie Smith, Nim Tharpe, Rusty Tomlinson, Franklin Adams.

Fort Valley High School:
1961 State Championship Football Team

Front Row, left to right: Tommy Tucker, Timmy Giles, Johnny Bradshaw, Jody Hardeman, Dan Harrelson, Phil Mullis, Rodger Nelson, Eddie Robinsette. Second Row: David Brann, Thomas Greathouse, Johnny Walker, David Joyner, Dave Hardeman, Warren Wall, Ronnie McDaniel, Al Bickley. Third Row: Coach Faircloth, Richard Lawhorne, Hugh Barr, Rusty Tomlinson, Nim Tharpe, Charles Vinson, Ray Pearson, Tee Faircloth, Coach Sims.

Peach County High School:
1978 State Championship Basketball Team

Front, L-R: Tony Harris, Alton Howard, Cedrick Allen, Brian Moore, Lopez Carter. Back row: Anthony Small, Marvin Dyson, Terrance Wright, Donald Walker, Quinton Small, Nathan Williams. Head Coach was Charlie Smith. Assistant Coach was Emory Lightfoot. Manager was Robert Tallart.

Peach County High School:
2005 State Championship Football Team

Front row (L-R): Christopher Slaughter, Udon Umoh, Chris Postell, Kip Postell, Kip Pearson, Duranzo Brown, Coach Rance Gillespie, Antonio Henton, Terrence Hatcher, Tony Davis, Terry McGhee, Rayfield Everett, Bryce Mackey (Mgr.). Second Row: Mareo Howard, Nick Manson, Keith Searcy, Shermaine Dickey, Brad Tooks, Desmond Jackson, Alex Byrd, Bruce Byrd, Brian Herrington, Wayne Williams, Reggie Taylor, Preston Battle, Donovan Howard (Mgr.). Third Row: Quintin Smith, Jaquez Banks, Courtland Roberson, Juan Rodriguez, Terry White, Courtney Harris, Keyon Slappy, Matt Deese, Nigel Talton, Kenneth Cryder, Charles Canady, Marquez Cullens, CJ Story, Charris Green (Mgr.). Fourth Row: Quentez Scott, Darrell Washington, Victor Neal, Greg Lewis, Shervarius Jackson, Brandon Thomason, Johnathan Tabor, Sam Whimbley, Anthony Howell, Antonio Wright, Stedmon Hodges, Arquavious Searcy, Justin Jones (Mgr.). Fifth Row: Bruce Mackey, DreQuay Everett, Keith Pearson, Jared Nelson, Patrick Wray, Dion Armstrong, Darius Raines, Wesley Hollingshed, Dustin Chancellor, Matt Nobles, Tanarius Warren, Jontae Lockett, Lamont Wray (Mgr.). Sixth Row: David Norwood, Marnique Williams, Matt Hight, Jaquez George, Marcus Meeks, Kameron White, Cornell Tucker, John Jackson, Justin George, Nick Bell, Tavarus Simmons, Sam Chester, Darion Howard (Mgr.), Keisha Richmond (Mgr.). Seventh Row: Coach Bernard Young, Coach Jeff Bell, Coach Todd Cooper, Coach Ricky Wray, Coach Bruce Mackey, Coach Jim Finch, Coach Chad Campbell, Coach Shawn Morgan, Coach Jeff Bailey, Coach Drew Fowler. (Not pictured: Jeremiah Wright, Dallas Christopher, Narada Moore).

Fort Valley High and Industrial School: 1929 State Football Champions

Players not identified in records. Coaches are at far right: Leroy Bywaters and Henry Alexander Hunt (with hat).

Coach Norman Faircloth, the famous basketball and football coach at Fort Valley High School, from 1949 through 1970, was one of Georgia's greatest coaches. Faircloth was enshrined in the Georgia Sports Hall of Fame in April 1999. His teams captured four state basketball championships, three at Fort Valley (1952, 1954, and 1961) and one at Cochran High School (1943). He was recognized by the Atlanta Tip-off Club as one of Georgia's winningest basketball coaches with 545 career victories, including a record seventy-eight consecutive victories at home. His football record at Fort Valley

Hall of Fame Coach Norman Faircloth, Fort Valley High School.

High was a phenomenal 124 wins against only thirty-four losses and five ties, including a state championship in 1961. Being a multi-dimensional coach, his track teams won twelve region crowns.

Note: Photos were not available for four other state championship teams from the Valley:

Football
Fort Valley High School-1948
H. A. Hunt High School-1958

Basketball
H. A. Hunt High School-1954
H. A. Hunt High School-1960

Chapter 22
Fistfight at Bay Creek: the rivalry between Fort Valley and Perry

The Rivalry during the 1930s, '40s, '50s and '60s

Rivalry in sports between nearby towns is normal and expected, but the rivalry between Fort Valley and Perry, over the years, possibly has been the most heated rivalry in state history. The rivalry that exists today pales in comparison to its intensity during the decades of the 1930s through 1960s. In those days, death was better than losing to the opposing school. Contributing to the rivalry was the fact that both towns had Georgia Hall of Fame coaches—Coach Norman Faircloth (came to Fort Valley in fall of 1949) for the Fort Valley Green Wave and Coach Eric Staples for the Perry High Panthers. In those days, because of the coaching genius of these two men, either Perry or Fort Valley would usually win the 3rd district championship and advance to the state tournament.

There are several views regarding the origin of the rivalry. History buffs trace its roots to the early 1850s when Fort Valley defied strong opposition from Perry–who didn't want the railroad–in bringing the railroad to Houston County and, in 1873, completing a railroad spur to Perry. Hard feelings erupted again in 1924 when Fort Valley, by a legislative act, withdrew from Houston County and created a new county named Peach County. Fort Valley's new independence from the Perry county seat fomented ill will; in fact, many citizens in both communities stopped talking to one another for years. Others contend that Fort Valley was slighted by political shenanigans that resulted in Interstate Highway 75 being routed through Perry rather than Fort Valley. While I-75 has brought growth and prosperity to Perry, Fort Valley businesses have suffered from the lack of interstate traffic.

Most observers, however, believe the genesis of the rivalry began with the fistfight in 1937 at the Peach-Houston County line on Highway 341 near Bay Creek. Of the six Perry boys who assembled for that legendary fight, only one is still living and that is Dot Roughton of Perry, who is eighty-six years old. Roughton was a star Perry player under Coach Staples during the 1938,

1939, and 1940 seasons. In addition to Roughton, the Perry group that assembled for the storied fight comprised John Webb, Donald Clark, C.A. Boswell, Horace Grimsley, and J. B. Hawkins, who later became Perry's chief of police. Only six of the estimated ten Fort Valley boys have been identified: Rudolph Cannon, Biddy Vaughn, Lowell Parks, Yates Crutchfield, King Mullis, and Joe Mullis. Few people except the old timers know what precipitated the fight. Roughton disclosed in an interview that the county line brawl was the direct result of an earlier fight between a Perry boy, John Webb, and a Fort Valley boy over the affections of a Fort Valley girl. Roughton said, "Only two people fought. The fight occurred on the street in Fort Valley. I got out of the car and refereed the fight. Someone called the police and the entire carload of Perry boys was arrested and fined twenty-five dollars each." From Roughton's account, the Fort Valley boy wasn't much of a fighter and the Perry boy was soundly beating him when the fight was stopped.

The Showdown near Bay Creek in 1937

With the Fort Valley boys seething over the Perry guy jumping out of his car and challenging their friend, a Fort Valley contingent assembled on the county line and sent word to the Perry group to meet them for a showdown. Roughton said the Perry boys found him in the movie theatre and asked him to join them. Fort Valley was waiting when the Perry group arrived, packed into one automobile. Since Fort Valley had about ten boys and Perry only six, they decided to pick one from each side to do the fighting. Roughton, who had fought sixteen professional fights, was selected to represent Perry. Fort Valley went back to town and brought Rudolph Cannon, the state golden gloves champion. Roughton and Cannon each weighed about 145 pounds. When Rudolph arrived, he asked, "Dot, what are we fighting for?" Roughton replied, "I guess it's because you're from Fort Valley and I'm from Perry." "Well, let's get on with it," responded Cannon. Cars were parked with their headlights illuminating the fight area. Rules were established that it would be a stand-up 'bear knuckles' boxing match. Biddy Vaughn, the Fort Valley police chief's son, was named the referee.

Dot Roughton in 2004 at age eighty-four.

For the next thirty-two minutes (referee timed it), Roughton and Cannon slugged it out on the shoulder of Highway 341 near a peach orchard. The fight ended as Cannon caught Roughton with a left jab that almost knocked out three teeth and, in the process, severely cut his finger on Roughton's tooth. Cannon was bleeding profusely, so they decided to discontinue the fight and take him to a doctor. When Rudolph got home, his sister, Uldene Cannon Pearson, was shocked to see how bloody and beaten up her brother looked. She said her parents were quite upset and, as they examined his wounds, Rudolph said, "You should see the other guy." Roughton said, "I was beat up so badly my mother did not recognize me the next morning." Roughton had black eyes, three loose teeth, cuts, and bruises. Yates Crutchfield, the only known Fort Valley survivor, now eighty-three, described the fight as "brutal." "Cannon and Roughton beat the starch out of each other. Neither boy would quit," added Crutchfield. "No one won that fight," declared Roughton. "In my life I have fought sixty-seven fights and won several boxing tournaments, but that was the toughest fight in my career. I would unload on Rudolph with all I had, and he would keep coming." Roughton reasoned that, had not the two fought instead of all sixteen boys, someone would have been seriously hurt. "Rudolph and I became friends," said Roughton. "He was a good man. I liked him." Cannon's sister, Uldene, who graduated from Fort Valley High School in 1937, remembers the event well and will never forget how bloody her brother was. That incident set the stage for even more intense rivalry between Fort Valley and Perry, especially in basketball.

**Fort Valley-Perry Barred from
Regular Season Play**

Over the next decade there were many classic battles between the two schools on the hardwood, but in 1949 the lid blew off when a Fort Valley fan and a Perry assistant coach got into an altercation following a heated basketball game at the old Perry gym. Soon after this episode, Mr. Ernest Anderson, Peach County School Superintendent, one of

*School Superintendent
Ernest Anderson*

the best superintendents in Georgia history, made the decision to stop playing Perry during the regular season and only play them, if necessary, in tournament competition. Mrs. Marie Anderson remarked, "Ernest felt that it would be best to suspend play until the ill feelings subsided."

1949, 1952, 1954, and 1955 Games

Weeks after the altercation in 1949, Perry again had to play Fort Valley (Ned Warren was coach), this time for the third district championship in Fort Valley's old gym on Riley Avenue. Perry came from behind 14 points at halftime and won on the outstanding play of Mack Peyton, Billy Gray, Ed Chapman, Seabee Hickson, and Bobby Satterfield.

In 1952, with Coach Faircloth at the reigns, Fort Valley won by two points on a last second driving lay-up by Richard Aultman, now a retired Methodist minister residing in Byron. I was a junior playing in that game for Perry. That year Fort Valley had possibly its greatest team. Its big guns were: Ed Beck, Pat Swan, Jimmy Thompson, Strib McCants, Eddie Merritt, Ted Joyner, and Aultman. They went on to capture the state title and finished the season undefeated.

The next year, 1953, when I was a senior with teammates Billy Beckham, Franklin May, David Gray, Joe Leverette, Tommy Mobley, James Logue, Jackie Miller, Martin Beeland, John Malone, and Billy Brock, Perry won the state championship.

With Ed Beck back in 1954, Fort Valley again beat Perry in the third district championship game in Fort Valley's gym and brought home another state crown, again going undefeated.

The next year, 1955, Perry beat Fort Valley in district tournament play led by Sam Nunn, Virgil Peavy, Bennett Mauldin, Percy Hardy, William Harrison, Jimmy Beatty, and Ed Beckham.

A year later, 1956, virtually that same Perry squad won the state championship. So you can see how these two towns were so intertwined and competitive in winning championships.

1962 Game

Before integration, the next and last time Perry and Fort Valley (defending 1961 state champions in both basketball and football) played basketball was in the semifinals of the state tournament in 1962. My brother, Dwayne Powell, Lee Martin, George Nunn, Dennis Fike, Ronnie Sanders, and Ronnie Griffin led Perry that year. Fort Valley's top performers were Tee Faircloth, Ray Pearson, Dave Hardeman, Dan Harrelson, Tommy Tucker, Ronnie McDaniel, Jody Hardeman, Nim Tharpe, and Herby Smith. Ray Pearson could not play due to a knee injury sustained in the 1961 state championship football game. Perry won the 1962 game by eight points (52-44) before a capacity crowd at Macon's city auditorium in the state's first televised high school basketball game. Veteran observers contend that Fort Valley would have won had Pearson been healthy. That essentially concluded the rivalry between the two schools during the Faircloth and Staples era.

All is Well That Ends Well

In summary, lasting friendships developed. Roughton and Cannon became friends. Mrs. Helen Faircloth stated, "Norman (Faircloth) and Coach Staples were the best of friends." Mrs. Marie Anderson added, "Ernest (Anderson) and Coach Staples were also good friends." And I became close friends with Mr. Anderson and Coach Faircloth after I moved to Fort Valley in 1959. The county line battle did not stop the Perry boys from dating Fort Valley girls, however, as Perry boys became notorious for stealing away Fort Valley's most beautiful girls and taking them to Perry to live. My daddy, Lee Powell of Perry, did when he married Margaret Braswell of Fort Valley. Billy and Ed Beckham did. Mel Tolleson did. Bill Jerles did. Buddy Andrew did. And I did when I married Beverly Davis, Homer Davis' daughter, except Beverly kept me in Fort Valley. Coach Faircloth was lamenting the exodus of Fort Valley's girls one day in a discussion with several of his Perry friends. Coach jokingly said, "It is a shame we have lost so many pretty girls to Perry boys over the years, and all we got to show for it is Billy Powell."

Chapter 23
Churches in the Valley

History of Fort Valley Churches:

United Methodist Church-organized 1840

The Fort Valley United Methodist Church, initially named the Old Pond Church, was founded in 1840 by Rev. Miles Greene and James A. Everett (Fort Valley's founder who married Rev. Greene's granddaughter in 1835) on land purchased by Everett in 1832. Located a mile northwest of town, it once stood in a field behind the present school bus barn. Historical records describe

Fort Valley United Methodist Church

it as "an unpainted, wooden-frame building with a door at each end, shuttered windows, and wooden benches serving as pews." In those days the men sat on one side and the women on the other.

The Old Pond membership moved to Everett Square in 1848 on land donated by James A. Everett (Fort Valley's founder) and Matthew Dorsey. Black worshipers began using the vacated Old Pond Church building. The new church was erected at the point where Central Avenue dead-ends at Everett Square. It was a rectangular building, capped by a large belfry, with a porch across the front. It housed a gallery so slaves could attend services. Its membership was forty-five males and fifty females.

In April 1895, the Methodist Church appointed Judge H. A. Mathews (grandfather of Beth Mathews Collins and Mary Mathews Humble) as chairman of a building committee to explore the feasibility of erecting another church and to raise $50,000. At the church conference in 1900, the proposal was made to buy land on the corner of Church and Miller streets, called the Simpson lot. After heated discussions, the proposal passed 75 to 54 votes. Several members expressed opposition and one member requested his name be stricken from the church register. The land was deeded to the church on September 15, 1900. Despite significant divisions in the church, the new brick structure was dedicated in 1901 and work completed in 1902.

Three structures have been added: (1) Sunday School annex completed in 1918, (2) Fellowship Hall and Chapel in 1954 (built by Homer Davis-Beverly Powell's father), and (3) educational building in 1967 (project spearheaded by Dr. A. Smoak Marshall) built on two parcels of property: Miller Street home site of Dr. Virginius L. Brown, bequeathed in his will, and the purchase of an adjoining lot on Central Avenue.

First Baptist Church-organized 1852

Fort Valley First Baptist Church

The Fort Valley Baptist Church was organized August 21, 1852, with seven members who met twice monthly in a downtown warehouse. Its first pastor was Rev. J. W. Attaway. The church purchased a permanent site in December 1856 at a cost of four hundred dollars. The new building was dedicated in 1858. At that time there were at least twenty-five Negro members. A second sanctuary was built in 1901 and a Sunday School annex added in 1909.

The early church imposed strict codes of conduct. Dancing was severely condemned and violators were cited to appear before a church conference. Members also were disciplined for excessive absenteeism. Expulsion and removal from the church rolls was the penalty for departures from the faith.

The second church, which faced Miller Street, burned in December 1935. Services were held temporarily in a former downtown theater and later in a building that became Strickland's Hardware. Worship resumed at the church while it was under construction (1936-46). A new brick building was dedicated on May 4, 1947. The church education building was erected in 1955, built by Homer Davis (this author's father-in-law).

Two churches were organized in 1959 under sponsorship of the Baptist Church: (1) Second Baptist Church with pastor, Rev. Ralph Adams, and (2) Society Hill pastored by Woodrow Dorsey. The church in 1964 deeded its Vineville Street property to Chamlee Memorial Baptist Church (formerly Second Baptist), and changed its own name to the First Baptist Church of Fort Valley.

In 1966, the church purchased adjoining property on

College Street and two lots directly across the street. In 2000, the church dedicated a new spacious fellowship hall and educational building.

Shiloh Baptist Church-organized 1863

Shiloh Baptist Church began on Union Hill with a small group of Christians worshipping under a brush arbor. Land was deeded them by J. R. Griffin. A small church was completed in 1863. The first pastor was Rev. Perryman.

A tornado leveled Shiloh on Tuesday, February 18, 1975, at 4 p. m. Rev. Morris Hillsman called a meeting the next day to make preparations for rebuilding a new church. March 1, 1975, was clean-up day as members, friends, and Robins AFB military personnel cleared the grounds. The church's foundation was laid on June 27, 1975. Church services were temporarily held in the Hunt High Auditorium. Pastor Hillsman recorded

Shiloh Baptist Church

The Rev. Morris Hillsman's family – Shiloh Clockwise: Morris Sr., Morris Jr., Gail Bailey, Kerry, Sharon, wife-Bernice, and little Yanata.

two albums *Please Don't Play with God* and *The Reality of Hell* to raise construction money. The present sanctuary was opened on November 30, 1975. The note on the church was paid in full on September 1, 1979.

Rev. Hillsman is Fort Valley's longest serving current pastor, with thirty-six years of service at Shiloh. Born in 1944, his family moved from Cordele to Fort Valley when he was five. He became a member of Shiloh in 1956. A graduate of Hunt High School in 1963, Hillsman became a war hero while serving with the marines in Vietnam. His helicopter was shot down and crashed behind enemy lines. Hillsman sustained injuries including a crushed ankle. He was ordained a deacon and licensed to preach in 1966. He became Shiloh's pastor on November 14, 1972.

Usher's Temple CME-organized 1866

Usher's Temple

After emancipation, in 1866, the vacated Old Pond Methodist Church building was given to black worshippers. At that time, black ministers were being licensed to preach and receiving training at Everett's Mission and Rev. J. C. Cotter's Theological Institute. Desiring a centralized location, black Methodists moved to a two-story building on O'Neal Street, formerly the Blind Academy, which became the Odd Fellows Lodge Hall and later Edwards Funeral Home. The upper floor was used for worship services, the ground floor for school purposes. The first ordained elder and pastor was Rev. J. H. Usher, after whom the church was named.

On December 31, 1868, the church purchased the W. E. Sloan property directly across O'Neal Street and located on the southwest side of the Southwestern Railroad. The Old Pond Church was moved by horse and wagon to this site, and Usher's Chapel completed in 1880.

Ten years later Usher's Chapel was consumed by fire. The congregation worshipped in the Odd Fellows Lodge Hall until the second church, renamed Usher's Temple, was completed in 1895. That same year Fort Valley State University was founded in Odd Fellows Lodge Hall.

On August 18, 1958, fire again destroyed the church–a wiring shortage suspected. Services were temporarily held at the Hunt High School gymnasium until the third and present structure was completed on October 30, 1960. Homer Davis was building contractor.

Presbyterian Church-organized 1872

In a meeting held at the Byington Hotel (later the Winona Hotel) in December 1872, the Presbyterian Church was established with fourteen members. Reverend S. S. Gaillard, evangelist of the Macon Presbytery, served as supply pastor. Services were held in the hotel, private homes, and other churches until a new church was completed in 1876. On land donated by Mrs. J. L. Byington, it stood on the northeast corner of South Macon (now Camellia) and

Presbyterian Church

College streets (site of present Sunmark Bank). It was built of lumber contributed by Glenn Visscher and with funds solicited by George Sturgis. In 1901, this building was moved to the east side of Miller Street, two lots south on College Street.

The present building on Central Avenue was erected in 1916 under the pastorate of Reverend A. G. Irons. The land was purchased from A. J. Evans, Dave Strother, and A. C. Riley Sr. for $900. The Session comprised Elders S. B. Wilson, J. L. Bozeman, and J. W. Woolfolk. The next year Emmett Houser and Will Brisendine became deacons. The longest serving members during the 1960s era were Cora Young Hallman and her brother Paul Young. Urbin Hallman currently holds the record, having been a member for eighty-three years.

Central Union Baptist Church-organized 1878

On June 26, 1878, a small group of parishioners from Shiloh Baptist Church organized the Central Union Missionary Baptist Church. The founders, former slaves, were Rev. Henry Felder, Rev. George Jackson, Alex Jordan, Deacon Wilson Wood, Bob Robinson, and Major Felder. Services were initially held under a brush

Central Union Missionary Baptist Church

arbor. Rev. Henry Felder preached until Rev. Ben Benjamin was named church pastor. The first church was a three-room wooden edifice built on the north end of Pine Street, circa 1880.

Groundbreaking began in April 1959 to build a new church on Preston Street. On March 27, 1960, the congregation marched from Pine Street to 501 Preston Street to dedicate the new building. By 1991, a spacious fellowship hall, additional classrooms, and a larger kitchen had been added to Central Union's physical plant.

Saint Peter AME Church-organized 1890

St. Peter AME Church

Saint Peter AME had its origin in 1890 when several members of the Bethel AME Church at Powersville began meeting at a brush arbor at Union Hill on the east end of Church Street. Because of the distance to Powersville, they felt the need for a church in Fort Valley. Among the pioneer members were Mr. and Mrs. Richard Hamilton, Mr. and Mrs. George Lightfoot, and Mr. and Mrs. Jim Basin. They continued to meet out-of-doors for a year before a church was built on the corner of Hiley and Church streets in 1891. The land was given by a Mr. Fairfax, known as "Blind Reed." This first structure was destroyed by a storm in 1895.

That same year, the second church was built on the corner of Hiley and Church streets when Rev. Wynn was pastor. The land was donated by Mr. J. R. Griffin for whom that section of town was named. The church was part of the Powersville Circuit of the Macon District. Bishop Abraham Grant was presiding prelate. In 1906, the membership numbered twenty five. In 1915, the church was rebuilt while Rev. W. E. Webb was pastor.

In 1936, Rev. A. J. Harris supervised removal of the church from Hiley and Church streets to its present location on State University Drive. The current church was built in 1971.

St. Andrew's Episcopal Church-organized 1897

In 1897, St. Andrew's Episcopal Church came into being as a mission of the Episcopal Diocese of Georgia. Its first building was the handiwork of a cabinet-maker, George Harrison, who settled in Atlanta four years after he left England. At the urging of Bishop Nelson, Harrison moved his wood-working business to Fort Valley

and set about organizing an
Episcopal congregation and
erecting a church building.
Bishop Nelson provided the
funds to purchase the lot
on Central Avenue. George
Harrison single-handedly
completed the chapel while
services were being held

St. Andrew's Episcopal Church

in the Methodist and Presbyterian churches. Exemplary of his
handiwork was an altar fashioned by hand from a popular tree.
Bishop Nelson asked Harrison to select a name for the church. He
chose the name of his old parish church in Uxbridge, Middlesex,
England: St. Andrew's.

In 1920, the little chapel so lovingly built by George Harrison
was replaced by a new building erected with timbers from the
original chapel incorporated in the ceiling and wainscoting of the
nave. During this era Rev. Dean and Mrs. T. C. Eberhardt, enroute
to make a church call, were killed when a train struck their car
crossing the tracks.

The twenty-seven-year ministry of Charles A. Robinson,
rector from 1972-1999, was a high water mark in church history.
Rev. Robinson endeared himself to his congregation and spiritually
touched the lives of many Fort Valley citizens.

Trinity Baptist Church-organized 1912

Thirty-five former members
of Shiloh Baptist Church organized
Trinity Baptist Church in 1912. Its
first pastor was Rev. C. S. Wilkins.
Services were held in the Mutual
Aid Benefit Hall.

Trustees R. T. Anderson,
E. D. Dawson, and Tom Slappey
purchased the site on State College
Drive to build the church. During
the ministry of Rev. J. L. Walker
(1924-46), the church building

Trinity Baptist Church

was completed. Through the aid of Rev. W.D. Reed and his First
Baptist congregation, Rev. Walker added an annex, doing most of
the work himself.

Rev. Julius Simmons – Trinity

During the forty-two-year pastorate of Rev. Julius Simmons (1957-99), the church's physical plant was greatly improved and the Anderson-Walker Annex dedicated in 1972. In August 1982, the church roof was damaged by storm, so services were moved to the annex. On March 18, 1984, the congregation returned to a completely remodeled church and a beautiful sanctuary. Rev. Simmons was a beloved pastor, a unifier in the community, and an outstanding spiritual leader.

Much of Trinity's early success was due to the harmonious functioning of the Board of Trustees under C. V. Troup, president of Fort Valley State College, and the Board of Deacons headed by Deacon Martin Edwards (Claybon Edwards' father).

St. Luke's Episcopal Church-organized 1940

St. Luke's Episcopal Church

St. Luke's parish had its origin as a worship and chapel center, first for the Fort Valley High and Industrial School (1913-32), and later for the Fort Valley Normal and Industrial School (1932-39). These two institutions, predecessors to Fort Valley State College, were financed and legally controlled by the Episcopal Church from 1919 until 1939.

When the Fort Valley Industrial and Normal School became Fort Valley State College in 1939, the Episcopal Church ceded the college to the state of Georgia but retained the Fort Valley Chapel and College Center and its surrounding acreage. Worshippers there petitioned the Bishop of Atlanta to recognize the center as a mission of the church. Consequently, in 1958, it was officially named St. Luke's Episcopal Church.

The present building on State College Drive, designed by Stanislaw Makielski, was constructed in 1940 through a gift from New York philanthropist Ethel Mary Cheney Thorne.

By history and tradition St. Luke's remains the university church with special responsibility for encouraging Christian ministry in the academic community.

St. Juliana Catholic Church-organized 1954

In 1952, Rev James H. McCown, an assistant pastor in Macon, also served the Catholic community in Fort Valley. He began holding services in the homes of Mr. and Mrs. William Khoury Sr. and Dr. and Mrs. Waldo Blanchet. Land was purchased on Highway 341 South and construction of

St. Juliana Catholic Church

a new church begun in 1953. The first mass was held in the unfinished church on December 13, 1953. Of the nine families attending this first service, Richard and Dorothy Scallan, William Khoury, James Khoury, and Howdy Thurman are still members. The church was dedicated on April 20, 1954.

The church was especially blessed in 1977 when the Sisters of Saint Mary of Namur established a small convent on Calhoun Street. The convent closed in 1986, but the spiritual gifts imparted by Sisters Joseph Marie Miner, Mary Charles Donner, and Kathleen O'Neill made a lasting mark on the community.

During the pastorate of Rev. Michael Burke (1980-83), a 2860 sq. ft. addition was completed in 1981. It included a fellowship hall, classrooms, office, and kitchen. Subsequently, the sanctuary's seating capacity was increased 40 percent. New pews and carpet were also installed.

In 1988, St. Juliana established a Migrant Ministry to teach English and provide social services to the large influx of migrant farm workers coming to Fort Valley to work in peaches. Spanish masses also began. Spanish masses now outnumber English masses.

The congregation celebrated its fiftieth anniversary in 2004 with over one hundred and ten registered families, including members from seven different countries.

Chamlee Memorial Baptist Church-organized 1959

Chamlee Memorial Baptist Church

Dr. Aquila Chamlee

The Rev. Mervin Watford and Dorris-Chamlee

The Second Baptist Church was born out of the Congregational Christian Church on July 29, 1959, with thirty-five charter members. It stood at the corner of Miller and Persons Streets (present 911 center). First pastor was Rev. Ralph Adams. In 1960, the First Baptist Church purchased the old Nazarene Church building on the corner of Vineville Street and Anderson Avenue (Citizens Bank site) and gave it to Second Baptist Church. The pioneer deacons were Wilkin Jackson, Thomas Jackson, King Mullis, Eugene Hutto, and Clarence Carney.

On March 3, 1963, the church voted unanimously to change its name to Chamlee Memorial in honor of Dr. Aquila Chamlee, a revered saint of the Lord who was president of Tift College (1922-1938). Dr. Chamlee and his wife, Mamie Louise Beck, retired in Fort Valley. Dr. Chamlee preached his last sermon there at age ninety.

In 1967, six lots on Knoxville Street were purchased and a two-story educational building with temporary sanctuary on ground floor constructed. During the spirit-filled ministry of Rev. Mervin Watford (1968-89), Chamlee experienced phenomenal growth in both membership and physical facilities: new sanctuary (1973), educational building addition (1976) and fellowship hall (1984). Watford, an accomplished sermonist, ranks among Fort Valley's most progressive pastors. Always giving God the credit for Chamlee's progress, Rev. Watford declared, "To God be the glory."

A children's wing was added in 1999 while Rev. Buford Tanner (1990-2000) was pastor.

Other Fort Valley Churches:

Fort Valley Evangelical, New Beginnings Baptist, Grace Baptist, Christ Anglican Episcopal, Gordon Chapel, First Assembly of God, Cool Springs Baptist, New Faith Baptist, Oak Grove Baptist, Richland Baptist, St. John Baptist, Society Hill Baptist-now Victory Baptist, Church of God by Faith, Church of Christ, Iglesi De Dios Ebenezer, New Hope Church of God in Christ, First Born Holiness, House of God Holiness, Liberty Praise Holiness, Fairview CME, Harris Chapel CME, Victory Deliverance Holiness, New Millennium Worship Center, St. Louis CME, Macedonia CME, Mount Olive CME, Mount Zion CME, First Church of the Nazarene, Bread of Life Worship Center, Calvary Chapel Heartland, Cathedral of Praise First Born, Church of Jesus Christ, Fellowship Temple of the Living God, Holy Saints of God, The Lighthouse, First Seven Day Adventist, Allen Chapel AME, James Temple Miracle Center, Greater New Fellowship Baptist, Holy Saints of God, Baha'i Faith, Kingdom Hall of Jehovah Witnesses.

History of Byron and Powersville Churches

Byron Baptist Church-organized 1845

Byron Baptists began worshipping in a brush arbor. Listed as a member of Rehoboth Baptist Association in 1845, they moved to a log building west of town on Moseley Road. The land was given by Joseph Harper and the building constructed by Harper, Ebeneezer Jackson, and a Mr. Leaptrot. Named Friendship Church, it also served as a school house. Its first pastor was Rev. C. Purifoy.

Byron Baptist Church

Byron Baptist (Friendship) Church reportedly was moved into Byron during 1880 and located on Academy Street between the school and city cemetery. The land was purchased from T. D. Warren for $32.75. The membership in 1887 was forty-six members. In 1950, the sanctuary was remodeled and twelve Sunday School rooms added.

Twelve acres of land on White Road were purchased and in 1974 a new sanctuary, twelve Sunday School rooms, and a fellowship hall erected. A Christian Life Center was added in 1983. Under the leadership of its pastor, Dr. Lawrence Kirk Sr., construction began March 2004 to build a new five hundred-seat sanctuary, a day care center for ninety-six children, and a new fellowship hall. The work was completed in May 2005.

Wesley Chapel United Methodist Church- organized 1848

Wesley Chapel, located northwest of Fort Valley on Taylor's Mill Road, sits approximately one hundrd yards from the Peach-Crawford County line. The church was established in 1848 when thirty-four members, including three slaves, began worshipping in a small log structure.

Wesley Chapel Methodist Church

In 1870, the Georgia legislature passed an act to deed two acres of land, including a log cabin, to the church trustees. The late Bernard A. Young, former Peach County Ordinary, who served twenty-five years as Sunday School superintendent, disclosed that the Crawford County Ordinary failed to effect the property transfer for thirteen years. Consequently, in 1883, the legislature re-passed the same order and transferred the property to five church trustees: Rev. Jefferson Wright, his son Benjamin, Thomas O. Vinson, Samuel Lowe, and Thomas W. Young (grandfather of Bernard A.Young and great-grandfather of Allen and Marshall Young).

The current church, a white frame building erected in 1923 while Rev. M. M. Marshall was pastor, is the fourth structure. The first two were log churches. The third was a more spacious building with two front entrances, one for men and one for women who sat separately during that era.

The current pastor, Rev. Gary Starrett, has served longer than any other pastor in the church's history (1988-1993 and 2000-2005). He also pastors the Powersville United Methodist Church.

Allen Temple AME Church-organized 1856

Allen Temple African Methodist Episcopal Church of Byron's Toomerville Community was established in 1856. Its first place of worship was a small structure (sixty-three feet long and thirty-one feet wide) which boasted a fifty-two-foot bell tower. The church was lighted by kerosene lamps and warmed by a pot bellied stove. The first pastor was Rev. Comwell.

Allen Temple AME Church

A cornerstone dated 1901 reveals that Rev. R. L. Brown was pastor; the trustees were J. P. Porter, G. W. Hamlin, R. Horton, H. M. Toomer, and L. F. Toomer.

The Rev. A. E. English led the church from 1958 to 1971. He currently lives in Macon and is 102 years old. Church Co-Chairman Sim Gibson stated that Rev. English was "a wonderful man, a community leader," and a "spiritual leader" who emphasized the importance of "casting a shadow for youth" to emulate. Gibson added that Rev. English has been called upon many times to preach funerals because "he knew how to relate to people in their loss and bereavement."

A new church was constructed during the mid-1970s. Rev. Willie L. Burner was pastor in 1987 when the mortgage-burning

Rev. A. E. English

ceremony was conducted by Bishop Frederick H. Tolbert. A new annex was completed in 1994 when Rev. Jeff D. Germany was pastor. Bishop G. K. Ming dedicated a new fellowship hall in September 1997 and assigned the current pastor, Rev. Charles A. Hicks II.

Byron United Methodist Church-organized 1882

Dating back to the 1840s, Byron Methodists and Baptists worshipped together in a log structure called Friendship Church on Collier Place. It served as both a church and a school.

Byron United Methodist Church

In 1882, the Methodists built a new church on South Church Street, and in 1886 the Byron Methodist Circuit was formed. It included Byron, Liberty, Wesley Chapel, and Shiloh (Byron's mother church, founded 1825). Jordan Chapel joined the circuit in 1903 and Powersville Methodist followed in 1920.

In 1922, a new two-story brick building (sanctuary and eight classrooms) was built on Railroad Street (now West Heritage). A youth center was constructed in 1947-48 and later enlarged through a bequest from the estate of Mrs. Mattie Kate Aultman. A new Sunday School annex with six classrooms was erected in 1958.

During 1966, a devastating fire destroyed most of the original church. A year later, in 1967, a new sanctuary was constructed and the burned church renovated as an educational building. To increase space prompted by increased membership, three adjoining parcels were acquired: lots of Ann Burnette and Morris Williams in 1984, the Post Office building in 1991, and Dr. R. C. Barnes' property in 1998, the latter converted to administrative offices. The Christian Fellowship Center (four hundred-seat auditorium and two conference rooms) was completed in 2000. Current pastor is Rev. Tom Nichols.

Byron First Baptist Church-organized 1892

Byron First Baptist Church

The church originated circa 1890 in the Tybee Community near downtown Byron. In 1892, the church split into two factions: Oakgrove Baptist Church, which located on Dunbar Road, and First Baptist Church, which built a small church in Toomerville.

A cornerstone reveals the second and present church was dedicated on November 18, 1917, and lists pastors: Rev. W. L. Peoples and Rev. J. L. Burney. Among the pioneer members were Emmit Toomer, Herbert Loften, Earnest Simmons, Dempsey Canady, Marie Gibson, and James Lofton, who donated the church bell.

Current pastor is Rev. Robert Bentley. The deacons are Chairman Willie Hill, Johnson Lee Collins, Louis Coley, and Johnny Maynard. From the congregation came two outstanding pastors: Rev. Charlie F. Richardson and Rev. Charles P. Gibson.

Hardison Baptist Church-organized 1902

Hardison Baptist Church was born out of a tent meeting in 1901 led by Rev. W. L. Cutts. On September 26, 1902, Mr. and Mrs. Jeff D. Hardison deeded the property, four miles west of Byron near Frog Pond, and the new church was dedicated on April 10, 1904. Five new classrooms were added in 1945. A fellowship hall, six classrooms, nursery, office, and kitchen were erected in 1959, and the sanctuary enlarged.

Hardison Baptist Church

During the 21-year pastorate of Rev. Boyd Dickey (1965-1986), giant strides were made in church ministry and facility improvements: sanctuary remodeled-1967, three story addition built (12-classrooms and nursery)-circa 1975, and new gymnasium constructed-1979. Rev. Dickey, a dynamic minister, widely known as the "Country Preacher," reached countless people for Christ through his radio ministry and through his missionary zeal in ministering to the un-churched, the sick, the shut-ins, and those in prison.

Rev. Boyd Dickey and Betty

The fellowship hall destroyed by fire in September 1993 was replaced with a new multi-purpose building in 1994. The sanctuary was renovated during 2002. Rev. Charles R. Odum is pastor.

Jordan Chapel Methodist Church –organized 1902

Jordan Chapel

Jordan Chapel on Giles Road west of Byron was founded in 1902 by William Jordan on land given by John H. Giles (grandfather of Fred Williams, James Williams, and Barbara Giles Ray). Richard Hardison and Walter Williams (Fred and James's father) hauled lumber from Macon by mule and wagon to build the church. First pastor was Rev. J. R. McMichael. Membership declined to five members and the congregation disbanded on December 4, 1994. The John C. Giles family still maintains the church and the adjoining cemetery (donated by Tom Jordan in 1892).

Powersville United Methodist Church-organized 1920

Powersville United Method Church

While the Southwestern Railroad was nearing completion from Macon to Fort Valley, a post office was built in 1846 at Powersville, named after Col. Virgil Powers, a railroad engineer. Since wood-burning locomotives would be passing through Powersville, a watering station was erected near the tracks. Soon a grist mill, saw mill, and cotton gin were in operation.

The first church in Powersville was the Allen Chapel Congregational Church. By 1919, its membership had risen to fifty-six; consequently, the decision was made to build a new church. Using a $500 loan from the Congregational Building Society of New York, land was purchased and a new frame church built. In 1920, the trustees decided to change to Methodism. After repaying the $500 loan, the Powersville Methodist Church came into existence.

In 1948, the men of the church, using a mule-drawn scoop, leveled an area next to the sanctuary. Sunday School rooms and a kitchen were added upstairs and a small fellowship hall downstairs. In 1990, a new fellowship hall and additional Sunday School rooms were constructed.

The Powersville-Wesley Chapel Charge has been selected the "Macon District Charge of the Year" several times. Powersville UMC was voted the "Small Church of the Year" in 2003.

Other Byron-Powersville churches:

Church of God by Faith, Springhill Community Church, Bethel AME, Lizzie Chapel, Little Union Primitive Baptist, Fairview CME, Mount Pleasant Baptist, Peach Christian Crisis Intervention, Byron Church of Christ, Faith Tabernacle, The Gathering of the CMA, New Faith Baptist, Lifepoint Church, Dayspring Baptist, Little Bethel Baptist, New Life Worship Center, Living Hope Baptist, Oakgrove Baptist, Abundant Life Baptist, and Harmony Community Church.

Chapter 24
Peach County Veterans

On December 7, 1941, Japan attacked Pearl Harbor. The next day President Franklin D. Roosevelt asked Congress for a declaration of war. As Dorothy Avera Hudson, her brother, and parents were finishing Sunday lunch–about 1:30 p.m.–the President came on the radio to announce that the United States had declared war against Japan. Dorothy said a pall of sadness and apprehension swept over the family. The Avera family had planned an entertaining afternoon affair; however, Dorothy's mother, Loyce, realizing the preciousness of being together, said "We are going to stay home today." Mrs. Avera knew that the worst was yet to come: that families would be separated as men went off to war and that the duration and outcome of the war was uncertain. Dorothy, born in Fort Valley, was living in Florida at the time. She said that within two weeks men were signing up for the draft at churches and courthouses. Out of patriotism, Dorothy attempted to join the Navy but was turned down due to a minor heart problem. She became a teacher instead. Her brother, Bill, went into the Navy and her father, Horace, went to Hawaii to help rebuild Pearl Harbor.

The Peach County Draft Board, which swung into high gear in December 1941, was managed by Mrs. Virlyn Wells (wife of D. Warner Wells and Neva Lowe's sister). Fred Shepard went off to war, leaving behind a wife and a two-year-old daughter. Fred's wife, Marian, commented, "It was a difficult trying time, but we made out the best we could." Fred stated, "There is no telling how long the war would have lasted had not the United States dropped the atomic bomb." Billy Marshall, stationed with General Paul Tibbets, remembers August 6, 1945, when the Enola Gay commanded by General Tibbets departed Tinian Island and dropped the atomic bomb on Japan. When the bomb was dropped, Buddy Luce, a commissioned B-29 pilot, was preparing to fly combat missions in the Japan area. Julius Shy Sr. fought in the fierce battles of the Philippines and Okinawa, and was part of the Pacific fleet that witnessed the surrender of Japan in Tokyo Bay. Kemper Hunnicutt, a bomber pilot, flew over sixty-five combat missions over Germany. L. J. Lomax fought against Hitler's armies in the famous Battle of the Bulge as allied forces crossed the Rhine River in Germany. Frederick Sammons, David Sammons' older bother, who served in the Army artillery, sustained a permanent leg injury during the invasion of Italy at Anzio and once had to swim through an ocean ablaze with burning oil when his landing ship was sunk. If the stories of all the brave Peach Countians who fought for our freedom were written down, this book could not contain them.

American Legion Post 76 in Fort Valley, commanded by James Earnhardt, recognized Peach County veterans at a special ceremony on May 29, 2004, the same day that veterans were recognized nation-wide in Washington, D.C. Herein is a listing of all known World War I and II veterans from Peach County. The list was compiled from four sources: (1) Peach County Service Record of World Wars I and II sponsored by VFW Post 6330 in 1948, (2) American Legion Post 76 records, (3) First 110 Years of Houston County, Georgia, 1822-1932 by the Central Georgia Genealogical Society, Inc., and (4) information provided by local veterans.

Tom Anthoine

Yates Crutchfield

George Culpepper

Marcus Hickson

Bill Hudson

Jack Hunnicutt

Mayo Lacy

L. J. Lomax

Martin Moseley

William Nance,
DDS, WW-I

Dan Nathan, MD

Roy Peavy

William A. Peavy Jr.

C.W. "Pete" Peterson

Fred Shepard

Frank Smisson

Francis Williams   *Hershel Williams Sr.*   *Allen Young*   *Virgil Young*
                              WW-I

World War II Veterans from Peach County:

Alden, John
Alford, Charles J., Jr.
Alford, William C.
Allen, Ethan C.
Allen, Newton Lewis
Allen, Otis Talbert
Almon, Carl B.
Alred, Lewis
Anderson, C.B., Jr.
Anderson, David Houser, Jr.
Anderson, George D.
Anderson, Murry
Anderson, Religh
Anderson, William J.
Anthoine, Julian P.
Anthoine, Marion E.
Anthoine, Thomas Robert
Ard, Tom
Armstrong, John R.
Armstrong, Lewis S., Jr.
Arnold, Joe T.
Arrowsmith, Charles W., Jr.
Arrowsmith, Frank L.
Arrowsmith, Jasper
Aultman, Hubert Anderson
Avera, Brown
Avera, Wilbur Kay
Avery, Hickson Woodrow
Bailey, Charles F.
Barfield, George W.
Barfield, Levi G.
Barker, Willie Joe
Barnett, Austin H., Jr.
Barnette, Gerhard G.
Bass, Earl Parks
Batton, John B., Jr.
Beatty, Dr. Earl, Jr.
Beckner, Edward L.
Beeland, Cecil
Bellflower, Austin L.
Bellflower, Charles J.

Bennett, E. Hale
Bennett, Escholl
Bishop, Dr. Barney Brannon
Bittick, Carleton
Booker, Bobby
Booker, Virgil A.
Borders, Andrew C.
Borders, Clint
Borders, Marshall
Bowden, Oliver C.
Bowden, Rufus F.
Bowman, Charles F.
Bowman, James R.
Bowman, Richard
Boyer, Harry W.
Bradshaw, Lester W.
Bragg, Henry Joseph
Bragg, Roger Joseph
Brand, George H.
Braswell, Henry W.
Braswell, Robert S., Jr.
Bright, Richard I.
Broadrick, George H.
Broadrick, George W.
Broadrick, John E., Jr.
Broadrick, John Elwood
Brown, Henry
Brown, James E.
Brown, John L., Jr.
Brown, Louis L., Jr.
Brown, Millard S.
Brown, Virginius Lynn, Jr.
Brown, Avera, Sr.
Brown, Louis L., Jr.
Bruce, Fain R.
Bruce, Ralph E.
Bruce, Roy J.
Bruce, Weldon C.
Bryan, Jasper Collier
Burke, Newton P., Jr.
Bush, Clinton C., Jr.

Bush, Maurice A.
Bush, Nathanial Arthur, Jr.
Bussell, Edward
Bussell, James Frederick
Butler, Dana A.
Butler, W. E.
Butler, Walter E., Jr.
Campbell, John W.
Cannon, Jeffie Rudolph
Carithers, Brown
Carithers, Floyd
Carithers, William A.
Carney, Clarence Joseph, Sr.
Carter, C. R.
Carter, Walton T.
Champion, Ralph
Clark, William D.
Cleveland, T. W.
Cleveland, Grover H., Jr.
Clifton, Ruth Lucas
Cochran, William David
Connell, James F. L.
Cook, Elgie G., Jr.
Cooper, Bud
Cooper, J. C.
Cooper, James Melvin
Crandell, Frederick R.
Cross, Frank L., Jr.
Crowe, Mack
Crutchfield, Clyde Yates
Culpepper, Alvah J.
Culpepper, George B., III
Cummings, Frank
Dasher, Clarence L.
Davidson, Joe E., Jr.
Davis, John W., Jr.
Demons, John A.
Dent, Hugh D.
Dent, Paul T.
Doles, Earl B.
Doles, Hugh
Donnelly, William T.
Duke, Jimmy V.
Duke, Julia Lynette
Duke, Leman P.
Duke, Victor L.
Duke, Edgar Lee, Jr.
Dupree, James C.
Dure, Leonard Carter
Dyer, Herman F.
Dyer, Horace A.
Edwards, John Thomas
Edwards, Thomas
Edwards, William Russell, Jr.
Ellington, Gordon

English, Bennie Almond
English, Dewey Wellington
Evans, Robert C.
Evans, William D.
Everidge, J. D.
Everidge, Thomas Vivien
Flournoy, Copeland W.
Flowers, Frank E.
Ford, Mark C., Jr.
Garrett, Billy
Garrett, Guffis Lafayette
Garrett, James David
Garrett, William Lee
Gassett, Elwood Jason
Giles, Noah A.
Goen, Perry
Goen, Ruth
Goetz, Nelson Fred
Goodlett, James Hopkins
Goodlett, Robert W., Jr.
Goodrich, Gus
Gordon, Kenneth Eugene
Goss, T. Bud
Goss, Thomas Merlin
Gowen, Edward J.
Greene, Miles P.
Greene, Pierce
Greene, Warren E.
Gresham, Frances B.
Griggers, Harold R.
Hall, C.
Halliburton, Shine
Hallman, Clinton, Jr.
Hallman, Edgar
Hallman, Leroy
Hallman, Lowell
Hallman, Urbin C.
Hamilton, Jack
Hancock, Watson
Hardeman, Wallis B., Jr.
Hardison, John Wesley
Hardison, William C.
Hardison, J. H., Jr.
Harris, Henry C.
Harris, Robert L., Jr.
Harris, Robert Ligon, Jr.
Harris, Thomas W.
Hartley, Jesse B.
Haslam, A. Worrill
Haslam, George Marion, Jr.
Hatchett, Bill
Hatchett, James Emory
Hatchett, John L.
Hatchett, Leroy
Hayes, Zack

Head, Harmon W.
Henderson, Conrad
Hickson, Marcus L., Jr.
Hightower, James Edward
Hiley, John Wesley
Hiley, Julian
Hiley, Lewis L.
Hiley, Mary Martin
Hiley, Warren
Hiley, Wesley
Hill, Flem
Hobbs, Casey
Holcomb, Jasper C.
Holland, Billy E.
Holland, Henry F., Jr.
Houser, Andrew J., Jr.
Houser, Claude
Houser, Harold
Houser, John A. III
Houser, Roderick
Houser, Russell P.
Houser, Wesley
Houser, William
Houser, John A., III
Houser, Andrea (Mrs W.A. Durfee)
Howard, Cecil
Howard, Leon
Howell, Homer Everett
Howell, Horace H., Jr.
Howell, Horace Homer, Jr.
Hudson, John William
Hunnicutt, George Kemper
Hunnicutt, Jack R.
Hunnicutt, James B.
Hunnicutt, Thomas R.
Hurdle, Leon
Hutto, Gene
Hutto, Willie Lowell
Irby, John J.
Isner, Melvin A.
Jackson, Edward P.
Jackson, George M.
Jackson, John W.
Johnson, Authur
Johnson, Edwin Freeman
Johnson, Jones T.
Johnson, Norris L.
Joiner, J. T.
Jones, Bill Tom
Jones, Edwin Thomas
Jones, George E.
Jones, James Calvin
Jones, James F.
Jones, James Frederick
Jones, Robert Meldrum

Jones, Robert T.
Jones, Roland S., Jr.
Jones, William Thomas
Jordan, Blakely G.
Jordan, Newt
Joyner, James Daniel
Joyner, T. O.
Kay, James B., Jr.
Kent, William Henry
Kersey, Francis H.
Kilgo, Clarence C.
Kilgo, Sydney L.
Kilgo, Walter H.
Killett, Alvin H.
Knighton, O. N.
Lacy, Mayo
Lamar, John B.
Lane, Doverd W.
Lanyon, Robert E.
Latson, W. Wilson
Lavender, Buddy
Lawhorn, Paul C.
Lee, Fred H.
Lee, Jack E.
Lee, M. Bruce
Liipfert, Bill
Liipfert, Jim
Lister, James E.
Little, Forester B., Jr.
Little, Garlan
Little, Garlin W.
Locke, Madison F.
Lomax, L. J.
Lowe, Graham Phelan, Sr.
Luce, Albert L., Jr.
Luce, George E.
Luce, Joseph P.
Luckie, Marshall Elton
Lunceford, Charlotte
Lunceford, E. E.
Lunceford, Hugh
Lunceford, Hugh A.
Lussier, Frances Wortham
Lynn, Richard R.
Mahmarian, John
Marchman, Robert L., III
Marshall, A. Smoak
Marshall, William Wooddall
Martin, Cecil Wilbur, Sr.
Martin, Marvin M.
Martin, Maurice Manuel
Mason, Calvin
Mason, John P.
Mason, Thomas P.
Massey, Linwood

Mathews, Aldean
Mathews, Benjamin F.
Mathews, Clifford J.
Mathews, Edwin F.
Mathews, George
Mathews, Jack
Mathews, Linton N.
Mathews, Robert Braswell
Mathews, Robert Lee
Mathews, Samuel M.
Mathews, Stuart Gordon
Mathews, Walter C.
Mathews, William Eugene "Billy"
Mathews, William L.
McCord, T. Ashby, Jr.
McGee, Earnest
McGrotha, Charles D.
McGrotha, Ross
Melvin, W. D.
Middlebrooks, George Alfred
Milburn, Charlie
Mills, George, Jr.
Milton, Cecil E.
Moody, Bill
Morrell, Rufus U., Jr.
Morse, Morton J.
Mosely, Martin Hood
Mullis, Joe
Mullis, King
Murphy, John W.
Murphy, William L. (Bill)
Murphy, John M.
Murray, Maxwell
Murray, Ramage
Murray, Russell E.
Murray, Thomas L.
Nathan, Dr. Daniel Everett
Newell, Willie Warren
Nichols, Coleman
Nutt, James Crawford
Ousley, Robert F.
Outler, Henry H.
Outler, Newton E.
Parker, William H.
Parker, Bill
Patterson, Cecil A., Sr.
Paul, Harold
Payne, Grady Robert
Pearson, James H.
Pearson, William E.
Peavy, Glen H.
Peavy, Roy Warren
Peavy, William Austin, Jr.
Peppers, Joe W.
Peterson, C. W.

Pittman, Harry B
Poole, Henry Gilbert
Poole, James W.
Prator, John W.
Pyles, Alton T.
Ransome, James Edward
Ransome, R. E.
Reddick, Harry C.
Reed, L. A. (Spike)
Rice, Eugene C.
Rice, Major B.
Ridgon, H. C.
Rigdon, Andrew Hill
Riley, A. C., Jr.
Riley, Howard W.
Riley, M. Brown
Ritch, Carl S.
Robertson, Benjamine L., Jr.
Robinette, Edgar H.
Rogers, Joe J.
Rouse, Robert L.
Rowell, Bill
Rowell, Deekin
Rowell, E. B.
Rowland, Lester L., Jr.
Roye, Frank J.
Rushing, Buford Claud
Sammons, Charles M.
Sammons, Clem H., Jr.
Sammons, David I.
Sammons, Frederick H.
Sammons, Ira G.
Sandefur, Edgar W.
Sanders, Audry
Sanders, Thullin L.
Sanders, Troy
Sandifur, Walter Lee
Saxon, John
Scallan, Richard
Schofill, John Luther
Schofill, Marcus Lynwood
Schofill, Otis Harold
Scroggs, Philander P.
Shepard, Fred W.
Shy, J. Carlton, Jr.
Shy, Julius T.
Singletary, Donald Lynn
Singeton, Louis P.
Slappey, Carlton K.
Sledge, Leonardis Patrick
Smisson, James Cliff
Smisson, Leonard Frank
Smisson, William S.
Smisson, Hugh F., Jr.
Smisson, James Clifford

Smisson, Louis E.
Smisson, Roy
Smith, Clarence Etan, Jr.
Smith, Harold
Smith, Jack
Smith, Leroy
Smith, Ralph
Smith, Roy A.
Snow, Louis G.
Snow, Willie L.
Spear, George W., Jr.
Spinks, Robert L.
Stephens, Homer D.
Stephens, Hubbard
Stephens, Marvin (Punch)
Stephens, Wallace
Stripling, Carl W.
Strong, Joseph J.
Summer, Henry M.
Sutton, Walter G.
Swain, Louis Allen
Taylor, Elizabeth
Taylor, Robert J.
Taylor, W. Sidney
Teece, J. P.
Tennell, Jimmy
Thames, Bill
Tharpe, Robert Carr
Tharpe, Walter B.
Thompson, Charles W.
Tomlinson, Victor H., Jr.
Treadwell, Draxton
Treadwell, G. B.
Treadwill, Jack L.
Tribble, Ralph
Tribble, Terry
Turner, Carl Harris
Tyner, Edrill
Vance, Charles S.
Vinson, Frank
Winson, John William, Jr.
Vinson, Charles, Sr.
Wadsworth, Carolyn
Walker, Brown
Walton, Claude V.
Walton, John L.
Walton, William
Ware, Emmett H.
Warren, Moultrie Alfred
Webb, Alva
Webb, Evelyn
Webb, Willis
Welch, James A.
Wellborn, Johnnie L.
Wellborn, William J.

Wells, Robert L.
Wheaton, George H.
Wheeler, L. Walstein
Wheeler, Lovard W.
Whitehead, William Adolph
Whiting, E. M.
Wilder, Harold
Wilder, James
Williams, Eddie Lee, Sr.
Williams, Francis M.
Williams, Herschel V., Jr.
Williams, James E.
Williams, Morris B.
Wilson, Emory
Wilson, Marion M.
Windham, W. L.
Wolfe, Lucius B., Jr.
Wouvis, Gus J.
Wright, George D.
Young, Allen
Young, Ed
Young, Hansel
Young, Virgil H.

World War I Veterans from Peach County:

Adams, Lev. B.
Adams, Willie
Akin, William G.
Allen, Charles
Allen, Howard
Allen, Steve
Allen, Will
Almon, Carl B.
Anderson, William J.
Andrew, Walter
Arnau, Robert L.
Arrowsmith, Frank L.
Aultman, Andrew
Avera, Benjamin Horace
Avera, Charles Holton
Barkley, Sidney
Barnes, Andrew
Barnett, Bell
Barnett, Lewis
Bartlett, Blanton I.
Bassett, Elisha Tansel
Bassett, Noble Paul
Bassett, Stephen A.
Bates, Oscar W.
Beeland, Johnnie D.
Bell, Clifford

Ben, Oscar
Benjamin, Clifford
Boddie, Henry
Boseman, Richard
Boskiale, Alfred
Bozeman, Isaac P. D.
Braswell, Henry Williamson
Braswell, Robert S. Jr.
Brown, Benjamin H.
Brown, George
Brown, Henry A.
Brown, J. L. Jr.
Brown, Louis, Jr.
Brown, Virginius Lynn, Sr.
Brown, Will
Brown, Willie
Brown, Dr. M. S.
Brown, Dr. V. L.
Brown, Earnest
Bryant, Loyd
Byrd, Luther
Byrd, Willie
Carithers, William B.
Chapman, Leon A.
Cheek, Earley E.
Cheeves, Willie B.
Clark, Hilliard J.
Clark, Ira E.
Clay, Willie
Coachman, Lindsay
Colbert, Willie
Coley, Jonas
Cosby, Essie B.
Culpepper, Bennie
Culpepper, Lawton M.
Daniel, Louie B.
Daniel, Willie
Davidson, William H.
Davis, Elijah
Davis, James A.
Davis, Nelson
Davis, Willie
Davis, Moses
Dean, Frank
Dennard, Arthur
Dinkins, John
Dorsett, Felix S.
Drane, Linizer
Dupree, Charles Lee
Dupree, Emmitt Jerome
Dwight, Albert
Eberhardt, Edward H.
Edge, Zeigler
Ellis, Collins
Ellis, Henry

English, Norman E.
Etheridge, Arthur P.
Evans, John
Evans, Love
Everett, Jackson
Exum, Walter Quince
Ezell, Sam
Fagan, Elbert Leron
Fagan, George Algie
Fagan, Roy
Farrow, Andrew C.
Fitzpatrick, Ben S.
Fitzpatrick, Nathaniel
Floyd, James
Gadson, Troup E.
Gardner, Lewis
Gary, William
Gilbert, Richard
Gilbert, Rufus B.
Gilbert, Russell
Gilbert, Willie
Glover, Samuel
Goodrich, Fred W.
Gordy, Lofton
Green, Sidney
Greene, Myles L.
Greene, Thomas P.
Griggers, Robert A.
Gunter, George A.
Haddock, Lucius Evans
Hall, Jimmie
Hall, Marcus
Hall, Robert J.
Hamlin, Albert
Hammock, John
Hardison, George O.
Hardison, Otis Walton
Hardison, Seaborn W.
Harris, Elijah
Harris, Henry Claud
Harris, James C.
Harris, Carlton
Hartley, Clarence L.
Hartley, Jessie B.
Hartley, Willie L.
Helms, John W.
Henderson, James
Henry, James Franklin
Hester, Irwin T.
Hester, Walton F.
Hicks, Roger
Hicks, Charlie
Hickson, Dr. Marcus
Hiley, Charlie B.
Hiley, David

Hiley, Warren L.
Hiley, Will
Hill, Claud
Hill, Josh
Hill, Lonnie
Home, Herman Homer
House, James H.
Houser, Willie W.
Houser, Charles M.
Houser, Russell P.
Howard, Johnnie
Howard, Leon F.
Hughes, Moses Jr.
Hunnicutt, James B., Sr.
Irvin, Eddie L., Jr.
Jackson, Bennie
Jackson, Isaac
Jackson, Johnnie W.
Jackson, Oscar
James, Lawrence
James, Ronnie
Jeffeson, John L.
Jefferson, Robert
Jessie, Arthur
Johnson, Alfonza
Johnson, Grover C.
Johnson, Willis C.
Johnson, Reese M.
Jones, Clarence V.
Jones, Edgar
Jones, James I.
Jones, Otis F.
Jones, Robert T.
Joyner, Robert U.
Kenady, Marchman
Kendrick, James
Kendrick, William
Kersey, Arthur Lee
Khoury, William, Sr.
Killet, Alvin H.
Kneece, Henry J.
Knight, Henry
Lamar, Jack
Lane, Lewis P.
Lewis, Isaac
Livingston, Boisy
Love, Arthur J.
Lovett, James
Lowe, McKinley
Lowe, Walter P.
Loyd, Burke
Lubetkin, Jacob P.
Lyons, Henry
Marshall, Ben Roe
Massey, Green

Mathews, George W., Jr.
Mathews, Lester
Mathews, S. M.
McAfee, Henry
McCook, Daniel O.
McCoy, James T.
McCrary, Charlie
McCrary, Horace
McCray, George
Merritt, Charlie
Miller, Charlie A.
Miller, Clarence
Mills, Marzells
Mitchell, William
Moncrief, Allison J.
Moore, Albert G.
Moore, Enoch C.
Morris, Will
Morris, Willie
Mott, Wilt
Murray, Willis H.
Nance, William Lambert, DDS
Pearson, Arnold H.
Pender, Charles H.
Peoples, Dewey
Perry, Charles
Perry, William F.
Pickens, James
Poole, C. B.
Rape, Wyatt L.
Ray, Johnnie
Reed, General
Rigdon, Hill
Rigdon, Irving
Riley, A. C., Jr.
Rowland, Lester
Rucker, Hooter
Rumph, Paul
Rumph, Willie
Russell, George C.
Rustin, John Wallace
Rutherford, Jerry
Scarborough, Ovid P.
Schofill, John H.
Sean, Willie J.
Shattles, Creswell
Simmons, Jim
Simmons, Otis
Simon, Gus
Singleton, A. L.
Singleton, Ira P.
Singleton, L. P.
Slappey, Anderson
Slappey, Ike
Slappey, Jacob D.

190

ᴊn, Hugh F., Sr.
ᴊson, Lewis E.
ᴊth, Eugene
ᴊith, Jerry
ᴊmithson, Joseph
Snow, Louis G.
Snow, W. L.
Solomon, James
Statham, Eugene
Statham, Frank Jr.
Statham, Jesse
Stevens, Howard
Steward, James
Stubbs, William Eugene
Tabor, Marison
Taylor, Lewis
Vance, C. L.
Vance, C. S.
Vinson, Rufus
Wade, Homer
Wade, Jesse
Walden, Ben H.
Walker, George T.
Walker, William Brown
Walker, Wilson

Walter, Thomas H.
Walton, Charles L.
Walton, Claud Vincent
Walton, J. L.
Wellons, Seymore
Wheeler, Durward Wilmont
White, Leonard
Williams, Herschel Venus, Sr.
Williams, Thomas
Williams, Walter
Williams, William A.
Williams, John B.
Wilson, Connie W.
Wilson, Damuel C.
Yaughn, Moultrie
Yaughn, Robert J.
Yaughn, Thomas A.
Yaughn, Willie L.
Young, Ed
Young, James M.
Young, Paul
Young, Sam
Youngstrom, Carl

then . . .
Fort Valley in the 20s

now . . .
Fort Valley today . . .